GHOSTS OF HOUSTON'S
MARKET SQUARE PARK

SANDRA LORD AND DEBE BRANNING

Haunted
America

Published by Haunted America
A Division of The History Press
Charleston, SC
www.historypress.com

Front cover image courtesy of Linda Pham.

First published 2020

Manufactured in the United States

ISBN 9781467141307

Library of Congress Control Number: 2019945073

Notice: The information in this book is true and complete to the best of our knowledge. It is offered without guarantee on the part of the authors or The History Press. The authors and The History Press disclaim all liability in connection with the use of this book.

CONTENTS

CONTENTS

INTRODUCTION

HISTORY AND MYSTERY SURROUND MARKET SQUARE PARK

I n February 2005, Debe Branning had just returned to Houston, Texas, from a five-day Carnival cruise. She was staying in the Houston area and was itching for historical-haunted adventures in the Bayou City before heading home to Phoenix, Arizona.

Debe found Sandra Lord on the internet and arranged for a private ghost walk on a Sunday afternoon.

Debe and her life partner, Kenton Moore, met Sandra at the Spaghetti Warehouse, then toured some haunted sites downtown and drove to sites that were included on Lord's tours, including pubs, an old hospital, and historic cemeteries.

Two hours turned into four, and a new friendship was forged between two ladies, who enjoy turning history and mystery into something special.

When Sandra contacted Debe to see if she had any interest in helping with this book, Debe did not hesitate. In fact, it was Debe who connected Sandra with the friendly and supportive folks at The History Press.

Everything in this book revolves around "The First Map of the City of Houston" from 1836, which you'll find on page 7. The name given to Block 34 on the map wasn't "Market Square." It was "Congress Square." Today, Block 34 is known as Market Square Park.

Chapter 1 provides a brief history of how Congress Square evolved into Market Square and eventually became Market Square Park. Because Sandra and Debe feel that, for some ghosts, eternal rest is impossible until their true stories are told, they have attempted to bring the ghosts who lived and worked around Market Square back to life in Chapter 2.

"A Short Guide to the Paranormal" explains some of the terminology Sandra and Debe have used in this book. Background details can be found in the Notes. Because the only thing in Houston that never changes is change, check out www.MarketSquarePark.com before heading downtown.

Let the spirits around Market Square Park reach out and make you laugh and cry and remember every time you visit the neighborhood where Houston began.

Opposite: First Map of the City of Houston, 1836. Courtesy of the Houston Metropolitan Research Center, Houston Public Library.

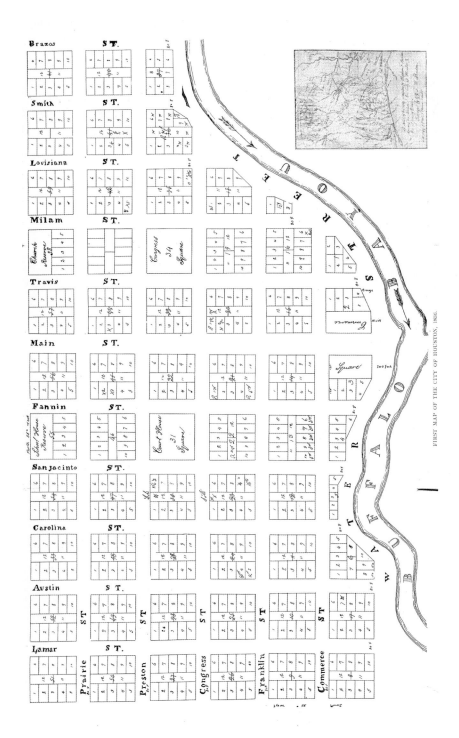

FIRST MAP OF THE CITY OF HOUSTON, 1836.

1

THE GHOSTS OF
MARKET SQUARE PARK

THE ALLEN BROTHERS

Augustus and John Allen were latecomers to Texas. Unlike most of the families who settled in Stephen F. Austin's colony in Mexican Texas between 1822 and 1836, they were not interested in farming or ranching. Instead, they were descended from a long line of speculators and land developers who had spent the last two hundred years moving from colonial settlements that hugged the Atlantic Ocean to virgin land in upstate New York in the new United States of America. Their ancestors had fought in wars and had been rewarded, not with money, but with land—land they quickly organized, advertised, and sold. Some of their ancestors stayed in these new settlements, while others moved on to land located over the next mountain or near a newly discovered river, speculating with their own money and the money of others who shared their vision.

Augustus Chapman Allen (1806–1864), the oldest of six boys and one girl, was a taciturn mathematician and scientist. John Kirby Allen (1810–1838), the third Allen brother, was more outgoing and charismatic, a born salesman. In 1832, the pair quit their positions as members of an investment firm in New York City and traveled south to speculate in Texas land on behalf of their family and other investors. Their goal was to establish a successful city in Texas. They finally settled in Nacogdoches in northeastern Texas, where they became acquainted with Stephen F. Austin and Sam Houston.

Top: Augustus Allen; *Bottom*: John Kirby Allen. Courtesy of Lori Betz.

As they learned about Texas, the brothers discovered that the town of Harrisburg was "an important supply center for Stephen F. Austin's colony."[1] Located at the junction of Brays Bayou and Buffalo Bayou, and not far from Galveston Bay, Harrisburg became a prime location for investing their funds and those of their family and friends "back east."

ROBERT WILSON

Robert Wilson (1793–1856) is a slippery ghost—or maybe just a shy one. There are no statues or paintings depicting him; we only know what he looked like based on the impressions of his contemporaries, who variously described him as tall, outgoing, gentlemanly in appearance and manners but with the rough hands of an engineer. He was also described as "a staunch supporter of the Texas cause…one who had, in fact, given his all in capital."[2] One biographer dismissed Wilson as "intriguing, but not particularly significant."[3] Another biographer "discovered that Wilson was far from unimportant in the growth and development of early Texas" but that "very little, if anything, had ever been written on him."[4]

Wilson was born in Easton, Talbot County, Maryland, on December 7, 1793, only ten years after the United States of America had been formed out of the original thirteen colonies. He was the oldest son of James and Elizabeth Wilson, who traced their roots back to Great Britain in the seventeenth century. After receiving a basic education, Robert was trained to be a carpenter and joiner in Baltimore.[5] When he married Margaret Pendergrast, the daughter of a Baltimore ship captain, in 1819, the United States already was experiencing unprecedented expansion.[6] The young couple soon sought new opportunities in the Missouri Territory, where their first son, James Theodore Dudley Wilson (1820–1902), was born on July 4, 1820. Next, they settled in Natchez, Mississippi, where Margaret died shortly after the birth of their second son, John Robert Wilson (1823–1855). As happened frequently in those days, after the death of their mother, the boys lived with friends and relatives until they could join their father in Texas in 1835.[7]

Water was the principal—and fastest—means of travel in early nineteenth-century North America. Most U.S. settlements were located on or near a body of water that emptied into the Atlantic Ocean and "within a day's walk of a river, so even the backcountry had access to the emerging markets that riverine routes served."[8] As hard as it is for modern readers to believe, river transportation was usually one way—downriver. Bateaux, flatboats, and keelboats were sailed, rowed, and floated from port to port along rivers like the Ohio, Missouri, and Mississippi. They were all dependent on wind, current, and oars. Large interior ports, like Natchez, served as *entrepots* or "gathering points," where incoming cargoes were sorted and consolidated before being transported downriver to New Orleans. From there, merchandise was shipped to Havana or Liverpool and beyond.[9] In 1820, there were sixty-nine steamboats on the western rivers; most of them plied the Mississippi. By the 1860s, thanks to men like Wilson, who knew how to build the wood-burning boilers and steam engines that allowed steamboats to make round trips, there were more than seven hundred.[10]

Perhaps it was Margaret's spirit that led her husband to strike up a conversation with William Plunkett Harris (1797–1843) on the steamboat *Mississippi* in 1823. As the two men watched the mighty river flow south on their northward trip that veered east to the Ohio River and Harris's destination at Louisville, Kentucky, he told Wilson about Harrisburg, the new town that he was helping his older brother John Richardson Harris (1790–1829) establish in Mexican Texas. Wilson, who continued on to

Bateau. Courtesy of Wikimedia Commons.

Baltimore, later remembered Harris as a "'remarkably modest and reserved man' and one with whom he was 'well pleased.'"[11]

The two men stayed in touch, and in 1827, Wilson decided to partner with Harris in the steamboat business. They were both "captains," accomplished river pilots, but Wilson was the "only one with any money and property." Harris contributed "his own acquaintance with the business and the people to contact." Soon, they owned a growing fleet of steamboats in Natchez that carried passengers and cargo on the Mississippi and Red Rivers between 1827 and 1830.[12]

HARRISBURG

In 1828, Wilson and William Harris joined John Harris in developing the town of Harrisburg in Stephen F. Austin's colony in the Mexican state of Coahuila and Texas. When John Harris died of yellow fever in New Orleans in August 1829, Robert Wilson defied the city's quarantine and procured the belting Harris had intended to buy for Harrisburg's sawmill and gristmill.[13] In June 1830, Wilson reported that "the earliest large manufactory in Harris County…does indeed perform well." It performed so well, in fact, that he and his partners, brothers William and David Harris, needed "smart, strong" blacksmiths to operate it.[14]

> *Either alone or in conjunction with the Harrises, Wilson had established blacksmith and turning shops along Buffalo Bayou south of the sawmill. There was a store, houses for workmen, and a lumber yard. His ships sailed to New Orleans, south to Tampico, and also up the Brazos and Trinity Rivers. Wilson also built customs houses for the Mexican government at Velasco and Galveston.*[15]

By December 1830, Robert Wilson and his new wife, Sarah Reed, a New Orleans widow who was wealthy in her own right, had moved to Harrisburg and received side-by-side land grants from the Mexican government near Clear Creek and along the northwestern edge of Clear Lake.[16] Robert's sons joined them in September 1835.[17] John Harris's widow, Jane Birdsall Harris (1791–1869), had arrived in Harrisburg with their oldest son, DeWitt Clinton Harris (1814–1861), in 1833. As John Richardson Harris's estate made its way slowly through Mexican courts,

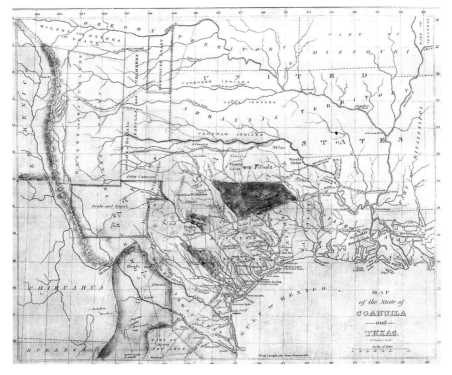

Map of Texas, with Parts of the Adjoining States, 1836. Compiled by Stephen F. Austin, American, 1793–1836. Engraver: John & William W. Warr, Philadelphia, active 1835–1837. Published by Henry Schenck Tanner, American, 1786–1858. Courtesy The Museum of Fine Arts, Houston, The Bayou Bend Collection, Gift of Miss Ima Hogg. B.69.264.

the ownership of Harrisburg became ensnarled in the Texas Revolution between Mexico and Texas.

On March 2, 1836, delegates at the Texans' Convention of 1836 at Washington-on-the-Brazos began signing a declaration of independence, creating the Republic of Texas. Sam Houston, one of the delegates, was appointed major general of the Texas army. He immediately left the convention to take charge of the army at Gonzales, sixty miles east of San Antonio, where the Mexican army, commanded by president and general Antonio López de Santa Anna, surrounded the Texan forces inside the Alamo.[18] On March 16, the delegates elected a provisional government for their new Republic.[19] The next morning, provisional president David G. Burnet, his cabinet, and many of the convention's delegates, including John Kirby Allen who represented Nacogdoches, left Washington-on-the-Brazos for the relative safety of Harrisburg. On March 23, Jane Harris welcomed

An Artist's Conception Of The "Cayuga" Steaming Up Buffalo Bayou

The Cayuga, Port of Houston Magazine, April 1981. Courtesy of the Houston Metropolitan Research Center, Houston Public Library.

Harrisburg, Seat of Government, Republic of Texas, March 23–April 13, 1836. Daughters of the Republic of Texas Marker Dedicated May 4, 1929. Photograph courtesy of Sandra Lord.

the men to her home, making it the seat of government for the new republic through April 13.[20]

Dr. Ralph Dittman's novel, *Allen's Landing*, imagined a scene late at night on March 23, when John Kirby Allen discovered his brother Augustus asleep outside Jane Harris's home, along with numerous other refugees. They walked down to the banks of Buffalo Bayou, sharing their impressions of what had happened since Santa Anna had destroyed the Alamo.

> *Then, looking up at the moon's reflection off the bayou, Augustus said, "I'll be damned if this water level hasn't ebbed and flowed just while we've been out here. Harrisburg isn't the head of navigation."*[21]

On April 14, 1836, Augustus traveled to New Orleans, where he raised troops and funds for the revolution. John, along with the cabinet, Jane Harris, and the citizens of Harrisburg, fled to Galveston Island on Wilson and Harris's steamboat, the *Cayuga*. When Santa Anna reached Harrisburg that night, he ordered it to be burned to the ground.[22] A week later, on April 21, 1836, General Sam Houston and the Texas army resoundingly defeated Santa Anna's Mexican army in eighteen minutes during the Battle of San Jacinto. The Republic of Texas became an independent nation.

HOUSTON

Dr. Ralph Dittman's novel, *Allen's Landing*, later imagines Augustus Allen telling Robert Wilson in the summer of 1836 that he had rowed a boat along Buffalo Bayou, west of Harrisburg, pausing several times to take soundings to determine the water's depth and the presence of a tide. When he reached the confluence of Buffalo and White Oak Bayous, he realized that the water was deep enough to allow small steamboats to unload and reload along Buffalo Bayou, then enter White Oak Bayou, back up, swing around, and return east to Galveston Bay and the Gulf of Mexico.[23]

> [Augustus Allen] *began, "You're an engineer, a sailor, and a steam man."..."At one time, part owner and skipper of the schooner* Rights of Man *and the steamboats* Ontario *and* Shepherdess," *Wilson interrupted in a rather flamboyant way..."not to mention having been*

master, at one time, of the steamboats Cherokee, Robert Emmet, *and* Lady Lafayette. "… "Well, do you think you could ferry a side-wheeler up Buffalo Bayou past Harrisburg?"* [Allen asked.]

Buffalo Bayou is unique. While most major rivers in Texas flow south to the Gulf of Mexico, Buffalo Bayou flows east from the Katy Prairie to Galveston Bay. As the area's weather history has made abundantly clear, inland settlements along the bayou are less susceptible to damage from hurricanes and flooding than Gulf ports, such as Galveston and Indianola.

Both Augustus Allen and Robert Wilson were well acquainted with early Austin colonist John Punderson Austin (1801–1833). Born in New Haven, Connecticut, "John found work as a sailor" and ended up in 1819 in New Orleans, where he joined Dr. James Long's filibustering expedition into Mexico.[24] He was captured by Spanish troops at La Bahia (Goliad), then jailed in Mexico City. After his release in the summer of 1822, he learned that Stephen F. Austin was also in Mexico City, waiting to receive a contract for his new colony. He contacted Stephen, and they soon became friends.[25]

On July 5, 1824, John Austin received title to 8,858 heavily timbered acres on a two-league tract in Austin's colony, which was located four miles west of Harrisburg at the confluence of White Oak and Buffalo Bayous.[26] He also established a home in Brazoria County for his Connecticut wife, Elizabeth Ellet Austin, and their two sons. After John Austin and his sons died from cholera in 1833, his father, the Reverend John Punderson Austin (1774–1834), traveled to Texas to settle his son's estate. In 1834, Reverend Austin also died from cholera. In his will, he left the upper (western) league of the land grant to his younger son, William Tennant Austin (1809–1874), and the lower (eastern) league to Elizabeth. Left without a husband and children, Elizabeth Ellet Austin married Dr. Thomas F.L. Parrott in 1834 and moved to Tranquility, his plantation in Brazoria County.[27]

In Columbia, Texas, on August 24, 1836, the Allen brothers purchased John Austin's upper league from an agent for Reverend Austin on behalf of his son, William Tennant Austin. Two days later, accompanied by their agent, Robert Wilson, they met with Elizabeth Parrott and agreed to her price of $5,000 for the southern half of John Austin's lower league. They closed the deal when Wilson handed Mrs. Parrott a $1,000 cash deposit. The deed was drawn up at the Parrotts' home on August 27, 1836, and was recorded on November 8, 1837, in the deed records

THE TOWN OF HOUSTON,

SITUATED at the head of navigation, on the West bank of Buffalo Bayou, is now for the first time brought to public notice because, until now, the proprietors were not ready to offer it to the public, with the advantages of capital and improvements.

The town of Houston is located at a point on the river which must ever command the trade of the largest and richest portion of Texas. By reference to the map, it will be seen that the trade of San Jacinto, Spring Creek, New Kentucky and the Brazos, above and below Fort Bend, must necessarily come to this place, and will at this time warrant the employment of at least One Million Dollars of capital, and when the rich lands of this country shall be settled, a trade will flow to it, making it, beyond all doubt, the great interior commercial emporium of Texas.

The town of Houston is distant 15 miles from the Brazos river, 30 miles, a little North of East, from San Felipe, 60 miles from Washington, 40 miles from Lake Creek, 30 miles South West from New Kentucky, and 15 miles by water and 8 or 10 by land above Harrisburg. Tide water runs to this place and the lowest depth of water is about six feet. Vessels from New Orleans or New York can sail without obstacle to this place, and steamboats of the largest class can run down to Galveston Island in 8 or 10 hours, in all seasons of the year. It is but a few hours sail down the bay, where one may take an excursion of pleasure and enjoy the luxuries of fish, foul, oysters and sea bathing. Galveston harbor being the only one in which vessels drawing a large draft of water can navigate, must necessarily render the Island the great naval and commercial depot of the country.

The town of Houston must be the place where arms, amunitions and provisions for the government will be stored, because, situated in the very heart of the country, it combines security and the means of easy distribution, and a national armory will no doubt very soon be established at this point.

There is no place in Texas more healthy, having an abundance of excellent spring water, and enjoying the sea breeze in all its freshness. No place in Texas possesses so many advantages for building, having Pine, Ash, Cedar and Oak in inexhaustible quantities; also the tall and beautiful Magnolia grows in abundance. In the vicinity are fine quarries of stone.

Nature appears to have designated this place for the future seat of Government. It is handsome and beautifully elevated, salubrious and well watered, and now in the very heart or centre of population, and will be so for a length of time to come. It combines two important advantages: a communication with the coast and foreign countries, and with the different portions of the Republic. As the country shall improve, rail roads will become in use, and will be extended from this point to the Brazos, and up the same, also from this up to the head waters of San Jacinto, embracing that rich country, and in a few years the whole trade of the upper Brazos will make its way into Galveston Bay through this channel.

Preparations are now making to erect a water Saw Mill, and a large Public House for accommodation, will soon be opened. Steamboats now run in this river, and will in a short time commence running regularly to the Island.

The proprietors offer the lots for sale on moderate terms to those who desire to improve them, and invite the public to examine for themselves.

A. C. ALLEN, for
A. C. & J. K. ALLEN.

August 30, 1836.—6m

The Commercial Bulletin, of New Orleans, Mobile Advertiser, the Globe, at Washington, Morning Courier and New York Enquirer, New York Herald, and Louisville Public Advertiser are requested to make three insertions of this advertisement, and forward their bills to this office for payment.

"The Town of Houston," *Telegraph and Texas Register*, August 30, 1836. Courtesy of the Houston Metropolitan Research Center, Houston Public Library.

of Harris County. One of the witnesses to the signing of the deed was Robert Wilson, who received a one-tenth interest in the lots of the new city as his commission.[28]

On August 30, 1836, an advertisement appeared in the *Telegraph and Texas Register* stating that the proprietors (the Allen brothers and Robert Wilson) were ready to offer lots for sale in their new Town of Houston.[29]

MAPPING HISTORY

According to Adele Briscoe Looscan, the granddaughter of John Harris, "the first map of Houston seems to have been made by G. and T.H. Borden and was used for advertising the new city." The Allen brothers and Robert Wilson, the proprietors of the Houston Town Company, hired the Bordens, who farmed the map-making job out to Moses Lapham, a professional surveyor. It took Lapham six weeks, beginning in October 1836, to survey, draw, and submit his map to the Bordens. It showed sixty-two blocks, most of which had twelve lots.[30]

On September 5, 1836, Sam Houston was elected president of the Republic of Texas, Robert Wilson was elected one of the two senators from the District of Harrisburg and Liberty, and John Kirby Allen became one of two representatives elected from Nacogdoches.[31] On October 3, 1836, all three men were present when the first session of the First Congress of the Republic of Texas convened in Columbia, Texas. On November 14, an act of congress "made the selection of a temporary site for the seat of government a subject of competition among the various aspirants…by joint vote of the forty-nine legislators in the two houses of congress."[32] Five days later, the *Telegraph and Texas Register* stated that the map of the town of Houston could be seen in the senate chambers at Columbia. A copy of what might have been that map can be seen on page 7.

The timing was perfect. Robert Wilson and John Kirby Allen distributed their new maps to members of congress as the City of Houston joined fifteen competing settlements for the honor of being the seat of government.[33] Allen and Wilson argued that Houston would be a patriotic choice. Their map showed that the street on the west side of Block 34 was named "Milam" for Kentuckian Benjamin Rush Milam, who, at the Siege of San Antonio the previous December, had asked his fellow soldiers, "Who will go with old Ben Milam into San Antonio?" Three hundred men had volunteered, including Robert Wilson. Milam was killed in action on December 7, but the Texans succeeded in capturing San Antonio and holding it until the Battle of the Alamo began in February 1836. The street on the east side of Congress Square was named "Travis" after William Barret Travis (1809–1836), the commander of the regular army of the Republic of Texas at the Battle of the Alamo. The street on the south side of Congress Square was named "Preston" in honor of William Campbell Preston (1794–1860), the U.S. senator from South Carolina who was one of the major supporters of annexing Texas to the United States against significant opposition in Washington, D.C. And the street on the north side of Congress Square was named "Congress Avenue" in anticipation of the capitol being located on Block 34.[34]

Because some of Houston's fifteen competitors had maps that also displayed patriotic street names, the proprietors of the City of Houston realized that they needed to up the ante. They announced that they were more than willing to help foot the bill for creating the new capital city. They said they would build the capitol and government offices at their own expense; in addition, they promised to donate to the Republic of Texas and to the Town of Houston five land parcels: Congress Square, the "Church Reserve" (Block 58, between Milam and Travis Streets), "Commerce Square" (Blocks 2 and 3 on either side of Main Street, between Commerce Street and Buffalo Bayou), "Court House Square" (Block 31 between Fannin and San Jacinto Streets), and the "School House Reserve" (Block 55, also between Fannin and San Jacinto Streets). As an added incentive, Robert Wilson, who owned Block 43, donated all twelve lots to Sam Houston, who agreed to lend his name to the town. That's why it is the only block on the map with no identification; it was never available for sale.[35]

The vote in congress still went down to the wire. On the fourth ballot on November 30, three congressmen who had previously stuck with the town of Matagorda through the first three ballots switched their votes, giving two votes to Houston, for a total of twenty-one votes, and one vote to Washington, for a total of nineteen votes. By a margin of only two votes, Houston became the provisional capital of the Republic of Texas. The cost of those two deciding votes: Lots 7 and 8 on Block 33, each valued at $500, were "donated" by the proprietors to representatives John Austin Wharton from Brazoria County and Thomas Jefferson Green from Bexar County.[36] President Sam Houston approved an act of congress on December 15, which declared that, beginning April 1, 1837, the seat of government for the Republic of Texas would be established at the City of Houston for a period of three years.[37] As they began selling lots, the proprietors of the Houston Town Company asked themselves what would happen to land values on and around Congress Square if it were dedicated to national government service for only three short years before the Republic moved the capital to another city. Many of the purchasers of the lots surrounding Block 34 opened businesses designed to entice farmers, ranchers, and planters to travel to Houston with wagonloads of goods to be sold in the city or shipped out from the landing at the foot of Commerce Square. Those same farmers, ranchers, and planters usually brought their families to visit friends and relatives in town while they shopped for supplies to load into their wagons for the trip back home.

Wisely, on April 7, 1837, the proprietors extended the boundaries of the City of Houston by one block on all four sides. A month later, the capitol building, which was located on the northwest corner of Block 57 and surrounded by Main Street, Prairie Avenue, Travis Street, and a brand-new Texas Avenue, hosted the second session of the First Congress of the Republic of Texas.[38]

WELCOME TO HOUSTON!

On January 22, 1837, three days after the first lot in the new City of Houston was sold, the steamboat *Laura* became the first vessel to sail from Harrisburg to the foot of Main Street. As its passengers discovered that the "city was still one of tents," the fourth Allen brother, Henry Rowland Allen (1817–1881), welcomed his brother John to Houston's only log house. Several small houses were under construction using logs hauled in from the forest, local lumber that sold for $150 to $200 per thousand feet, or lumber shipped in from Maine.[39]

Late at night on March 3, 1837, as his last act on his last day as president of the United States, Andrew Jackson formally recognized the Republic of Texas, a step that encouraged more Americans to become Texans. A month later, President Sam Houston, the government, and the republic's archives arrived overland from Columbia, while the steamboat *Yellow Stone* unloaded members of congress and the *Telegraph and Texas Register*'s new printing press at the Commerce Square Landing.[40]

By May 7, 1837, Houston was reported to have 1,200 inhabitants. Many of the new residents were forced to sleep under tents or inside barrels,

Navigating Buffalo Bayou in Early Days

The Laura, R.M. Farrar, The Story of Buffalo Bayou and the Houston Ship Channel. (Houston, Texas: Chamber of Commerce, 1926) 5. Courtesy of the Houston Metropolitan Research Center, Houston Public Library.

while others simply camped on the open prairie. There were no sanitation facilities—not even an outhouse. Luckily, when Charlotte Marie Baldwin Allen (1805–1895), the wife of Augustus Allen, arrived in Houston, her brother-in-law Henry exhibited southern chivalry by moving his tenants out of their log house so that Charlotte could live in relative comfort until her own house was completed.[41]

The republic's charter authorized the citizens of Houston to elect officers, including a mayor; up to eight aldermen; a secretary and treasurer; a tax collector; and a constable.[42] James Sanders Holman (1804–1864), an agent for the proprietors of the Houston Town Company, won the city's first election for mayor on August 14, 1837. Two days earlier, Holman had written that "up to this time, the sales of town lots amount to upwards of two hundred thousand dollars, and every day is rapidly increasing the amount." In November 1837, the proprietors inventoried all Houston land that had not been previously sold and held a public sale, which continued until December 11, 1837, when an investor named Angus McNeill purchased all 303 lots for $80,000.[43]

Charlotte Marie Baldwin Allen and Daughter. Courtesy of the Houston Metropolitan Research Center, Houston Public Library.

When John Allen dissolved his partnership with Augustus Allen and Robert Wilson on June 16, 1838, in order to pursue interests in Nacogdoches and start an import-export venture between Texas and England, the new owners of the Houston Town Company—McNeill, Allen, and Holman, with Augustus as controlling partner—possessed less than half of the land that the Houston Town Company had owned in August 1836.[44] Two months later, on August 15, 1838, John Allen died of congestive fever—probably malaria or yellow fever—in Augustus's Houston home. Because John died without a will, his brother Henry was appointed administrator of the estate, which was appraised at $814,662. The probate court's costs and fees, which equaled $4,073.31, or one-half of one percent of the estate's appraised value, were to be paid by Augustus. Augustus, however, had become president of the City of Brazos Company, which was promoting a new town fifty-three miles northwest of Houston. In July 1840, he had begun building a railroad to connect Houston to Brazos, but the company had failed. He was broke.[45]

Between 1839 and 1840, William Robinson Baker, the probate court judge and the Allen brothers' former clerk, issued seven arrest orders for Augustus because of his refusal to pay the court's costs and fees. Finally, he was jailed without bail in September 1840 and forced to report on the succession of the partnership. "With slashing strokes, Augustus angrily wrote what he called a clarification of the matter of succession." His father, Rowland Allen III (1781–1843), and mother, Sally Chapman Allen (1787–1841), were first in line to inherit John's estate. Following their deaths, the remaining Allen brothers—Samuel (1808–1895), Henry (1817–1881), George (1815–1854), and Harvey (1819–1862)—would inherit their respective shares.[46]

Augustus left Houston in 1842 to volunteer with the Texas army as it drove General Adrian Woll and his 1,200 Mexican troops from San Antonio. He returned after his father's death in 1843 and "began the tedious process of winding up his real estate business," which was made more complicated by the fact that some of the money the brothers had used in their earlier enterprises had come from an inheritance left to Charlotte by her father, Dr. Jonas Baldwin, before her marriage and from property belonging to other members of the Baldwin family.[47]

In 1848, on the advice of his physician, Augustus moved south to Brownsville, hoping to improve his failing health. While there, he was appointed deputy collector of customs. When he returned to Houston in 1850, Charlotte announced that she was so "dissatisfied with the methods being employed in the settlement" of the business that she wanted "a separation, without divorce," from her husband. They successfully "pledged to keep the details of their troubles secret."[48]

Augustus left Houston after signing over to Charlotte "the bulk of what remained of his many enterprises." He moved to Mexico, where he secured valuable timber concessions and soon amassed another fortune. In 1852, the United States appointed him consul for the port of Tehuantepec on the Pacific Ocean and, in 1858, to a similar post for the port of Minotitlán, giving him "control of the consular affairs of the United States for the entire Isthmus of Tehuantepec, a commercially important position, since a trade route—probably a canal—through that region" was being contemplated.[49]

By 1864, when it became clear that Augustus was never going to recover his health, "he closed his private business and went to Washington, D.C., to resign his consulships." He contracted pneumonia soon after arriving and died on June 11, 1864. The Civil War was raging, and access to Galveston was blocked by the Union navy. There was no way to transport Augustus's remains from Washington to Houston. On August 29, 1864, twenty-eight years after founding the City of Houston, Augustus was buried in Green-

Wood Cemetery in Brooklyn, New York.[50] Charlotte remained in Houston for the next thirty-one years and became one of the city's best-known citizens. She sported her own cattle brand and was considered "uncommonly successful in business for a woman." When she died at the age of ninety on August 3, 1895, Houstonians observed a day of mourning.[51]

The litigation over who originally owned what in Houston has provided years of billable hours for local law firms.

THE CITY RECESS

Before Market Square housed Houston's first four City Halls, it was a construction staging area. Mexican soldiers captured at the Battle of San Jacinto were brought into Houston to help slaves and free men of color cut down the trees on Block 34. Unfortunately, most of the logs were useless because the sawmill in Harrisburg had been destroyed by Santa Anna's army in April 1836. With permission from John Kirby Allen, master carpenter Robert Prettyman Boyce (1814–1888) dug a "sawpit" at the corner of Milam and Congress Streets on Block 34. He also ordered a whipsaw from New Orleans. Whipsaws were usually from five to seven feet long and required one man to stand in the excavated pit while the other mounted a scaffold in order to cut the tree trunk into long boards.[52] The next time you walk along the Congress Street side of Market Square Park in the spring or fall, your scratchy eyes and froggy throat may not be the result of hay fever; they may come from sawdust that still hangs invisibly in the air.

Soon after it was elected, Houston's first City Council passed an ordinance that made private competition illegal for anyone selling "meat, fish, fowl, or vegetables at any other place than the market house of the city during market hours"—from 4:00 to 9:00 a.m. during the winter and from 5:00 to 10:00 a.m. during the summer. To accommodate vendors, the City Council also ordered the construction of a "city recess," which was located in the center of Market Square, with entrances and exits facing Travis Street to the east and Milam Street to the west.[53] It was a large, one-story wooden shed with stalls lining each side of a central dirt walkway. Merchants like C. Kelly quickly secured a stall and offered for sale "the following articles, low for cash: coffee, spice, liquors of all kinds; porter; spectacles; calicoes; all kinds of thread; and shoes, hats, and ready made clothing; carpenter's tools of all descriptions."[54]

Market Place, Houston, Texas, March 20th, 1852. Thomas Flintoff
Houston's First City Hall
Original watercolor courtesy of Houston Metropolitan Research Center, Houston Public Library.

Thomas Flintoff, Market Place and Gaol, Houston, Texas, March 20th, 1852. Original watercolor courtesy of the Houston Metropolitan Research Center, Houston Public Library.

The city recess was under the control of the city's market inspector, Thomas F. Gravis. At first, Gravis was paid one-half of the market fees collected. Later, "when he found that one-half was not enough for his support, he asked for and was given all the fees." His job was to keep the public market "neat and clean" with the assistance of a group of pigs who roamed the area freely. In 1841, the City Council made the position of market master so valuable that there were ten applicants. In 1845, the duties of market master and city marshal were combined.[55]

HOUSTON'S FIRST CITY HALL, 1841–1872

On September 20, 1840, Houston's City Council decided to replace the city recess with a permanent, rectangular-shaped, one-story, wood-frame building facing Travis Street at a cost of $1,200. It included vendor stalls on either side of a dirt walkway and new permanent canopies supported by simple wood posts.[56] Not long after they awarded the construction contract to Thomas Stansbury & Sons, the members of City Council, who had been meeting in Kessler's arcade, a saloon one-half block away on Travis Street, amended the contract to include an adjoining two-story structure with a pitched roof to the east of the marketplace. The upper story was used as Houston's first City Hall and police court, while the lower story held the city jail. Stansbury & Sons' final bill was $8,000. The additional money must have been worth it because the wood-frame complex, which was completed in November 1841, lasted for thirty-one years.[57]

After the city built its first bridge across Buffalo Bayou at Preston Street in 1848, Market Square became "a noisy, teeming place that encouraged businessmen to purchase sites for their stores," filling in the blocks surrounding Market Square with one- and two-story wood-frame buildings.[58] In Thomas Flintoff's 1852 watercolor, the Market House is on the left, while City Hall and the city jail are located in the smaller building on the right. Notice the tower rising out of the center of City Hall's roof; it was replaced in 1860 with a combination bell and clock tower. The bell was used to give fire alarms, announce important gatherings and events, and toll the curfew at 9:00 p.m. each night. Historians write that life was good in Houston in 1860; it was the "best commercial year she had ever seen," despite "[m]uddy streets, mosquitoes, and yellow fever epidemics," no paid firemen, no paved streets, no covered sewers, no street lighting, no permanent health board, and no municipal services.[59]

Wood-frame buildings were gradually replaced with two- and three-story brick buildings, complete with canopies over their sidewalks to protect passersby from Houston's hot sun and driving rains. As in other southern cities, Houston's agriculture boomed, but with only fifteen companies, manufacturing lagged far behind the industrial development in northern cities.[60] Aided by generous loans from the State of Texas, business leaders began the city's economic transition from a regional overland and riverine distribution center to a railroad hub integrated with the national system. By the end of 1860, six railway companies had built 392 miles of track in Texas; five of those six railways passed through Houston.[61]

In December 1860, Texas Governor Sam Houston addressed a large crowd in Houston and urged them not to vote to secede from the United States of America. On March 2, 1861, Texas rejected Houston's plea and joined the Confederate States of America. Lieutenant Governor Edward Clark replaced Houston as governor on March 18, 1861. Houston died at his home in Huntsville on August 11, 1863.

Galveston refugees flooded into Houston after Union forces occupied the island on October 9, 1862. Although Confederate General John Bankhead Magruder retook Galveston on New Year's Day 1863, the end of the Confederacy in Texas arrived two years later, on June 2, 1865, when he and Confederate General E. Kirby Smith formally surrendered Texas to Union Brigadier General E.J. Davis aboard the USS *Fort Jackson*.[62] By the end of the month, Union soldiers moved into Houston. On July 7, 1865, one newspaper rejoiced, "Our city is rapidly beginning to look as busy as in former years. Nearly all the stores are open, and many of them seem to have good stocks of goods on hand." But it lamented, "[The] old rat promenade called the market house is a disgrace to the city and should be at once pulled down."[63]

Politically, the transition was not easy. Three acts of the United States Congress redefined what it meant to be a citizen. The Civil Rights Act of 1866 considered all persons born in the United States, including former slaves, to be citizens. The Fourteenth Amendment, which was ratified on July 9, 1868, guaranteed citizenship to "all persons born or naturalized in the United States." The Amendment's equal protection clause also guaranteed that no state could "deny to any person within its jurisdiction the equal protection of the laws." The Fifteenth Amendment, which was passed by Congress on February 26, 1869, reinforced the Fourteenth Amendment by providing that the "right of citizens of the United States to vote shall not be denied or abridged by the United States or by any state on account of race, color, or previous condition of servitude."[64]

Not satisfied with "Presidential Reconstruction," as it was carried out by Abraham Lincoln and Andrew Johnson, the U.S. Congress passed new Reconstruction Acts on March 2, 1867. One act divided the South into military districts and placed the former Confederate states under martial law pending their adoption of constitutions that guaranteed civil liberties to former slaves. Houston was part of the Fifth Military District of Texas and Louisiana.[65] While the "Ku Klux Klan appeared in town under a variety of more public names that sounded like social or athletic clubs…[t]he main concern of the former-Confederate whites was that they were, for a while, not allowed to vote."[66]

Alexander McGowan (1817–1893), the owner of the Houston Iron and Brass Foundry, became Houston's mayor for the second time in December 1867.[67] When Houston was unable to pay its municipal employees in 1868, General J.J. Reynolds, commander of the Fifth Military District, removed McGowan and appointed Joseph Robert Morris (1828–1885) to the position. Morris was "a substantial, well-liked conservative Republican who owned a hardware store" on Main Street. At the same time, Thomas "Timothy" Howe Scanlan (1832–1906), a moderate Republican, was appointed as one of the two aldermen for the Third Ward.[68] To generate income, the City Hall and City Market complex was leased to a Mr. McGregor in 1869. From then on, the city surrendered all control over the City Market to private individuals in exchange for rent. Unfortunately, Houston's "[m]unicipal records were destroyed while federal officers occupied the building."[69]

Following the November 30, 1869 state election, General E.J. Davis, who had the backing of President U.S. Grant, became governor, and a new state constitution was ratified. Martial law ended, as Texas was readmitted to the Union on March 30, 1870. Houston remained under state-appointed government until it received a new charter on August 18, 1870. In the meantime, Governor Davis removed Morris as Houston's mayor on July 28, 1870, and appointed T.H. Scanlan in his place.[70]

City Council had discussed replacing City Hall since the end of the Civil War. As late as June 1871, after Houston's municipal government had moved into Gray's Building on Fannin Street, across from Courthouse Square, "the city s architect was still working on the plans....Council evidently felt that no bidders could be found in Houston [because], on June 17, it authorized the mayor to go to New York, at the city's expense, to contract for the building of the market house."[71]

Between July and August 1871, Scanlan traveled from Houston to New York, accompanied by "a competent engineer," a recent Harvard graduate named Charles Emerson Hoar (1850–1912). Their mission was "to examine and report on pavements and other city improvements" and on how other cities "were coping with the need to modernize."[72] While Scanlan was gone, the first City Hall was torn down. Its clock and fire bell were put into storage until they could be installed in the new building.[73]

Scanlan returned from his trip in September and presented "an analysis of the mechanics of urban growth and progress" at a public meeting. He reported that as a result of the city's "unblemished record of meeting... semiannual interest payments" on municipal bonds, New York capitalists had Texas "on the brain." These Wall Street investors, he said, "viewed Houston as a solid credit risk, especially since the town stood at the gateway to a region that was undergoing tremendous immigration and expansion." Scanlan recommended that Houstonians have "the same confidence in its growth and prosperity that many sagacious capitalists and business men outside of Texas have" and improve the city with "asphalt paving, iron bridges, parks, and a new city market." One of Scanlan's comments was especially prescient: "The day is not far distant which will see Houston the Chicago of the South."[74]

In October 1871, both the mayor and City Council rejected an ironclad building, which could have cost as much as $250,000, in favor of a brick one, which had an estimated cost of $228,000. The construction contract was awarded to Houston brickmaker and builder William Brady during the third week of November. It was financed by both a $250,000 municipal bond at eight percent interest for twenty-five years and a continuation of the building's lease.[75] Brady's superintendents for the job were William Fleig and Robert Boyce.[76] The Brady Brick Works were located on the banks of Buffalo Bayou at its intersection with Brays Bayou. The soil there produced a "roseate-pink" brick. While the 1873 City Hall is long gone, visitors can still view Brady's bricks on Lovett Hall and Howard Keck Hall, formerly the Chemistry Building, at Rice University.[77]

In his September 1871 report, Mayor Scanlan also explained that a system of drains and sanitary sewers was a prerequisite to street paving with hard surfaces such as asphalt and stone. The subsequent cost of protecting Market Square from storm damage and supplying the new government and market complex with sewers was $100,000.[78] On February 1, 1872, the *Daily Telegraph* announced that prisoners were escaping from the city jail "simply by knocking planks loose with their fists."[79] It was time to replace the "old rat promenade." Charles Emerson Hoar was hired as the city engineer in February 1872 with an annual salary of $2,000. His assignment: modernize Houston.[80]

HOUSTON'S SECOND CITY HALL, 1873–1876

Shaped like a Greek cross, Houston's second City Hall had the simplicity of Italianate style and massing along with several hallmarks of the French Second Empire style: two Mansard roofs accented by dormers, stone window arches contrasted with brick walls, hood moldings and doors, and bracketed and denticulated cornices. Like the first City Hall, the public marketplace was on the ground floor. City government offices were on the second and third floors. The pavilions on the north and south sides of the building were new. The first floor was paved with flagstones and contained fifty-six stalls. The second floor was home to a council chamber, an assembly room, eight offices on each of the building's wings, a city recorder's office, a committee room adjoining the council chamber, and two parallel hallways. On the third floor, there were eight offices for city officials. A balcony that was seventy feet long looked out over Travis Street and was designed to accommodate addresses for mass meetings.[81]

Brady's crew began working on the new City Hall on February 28, 1872. It wasn't long before one disaster after another reared its ugly head. Brady quickly discovered that the architectural plans and specifications were "scarcely more than in skeleton form." Some rooms had no floors; others had no plastering or windows; provisions for blinds or shades were nonexistent; and there was no stairway between the first and second stories. As these errors were being corrected, Mayor Scanlan and City Council decided to add a one-thousand-seat amphitheater, complete with fluted columns and crystal chandeliers, to the second floor. The addition of this "Academy of Music" brought the final cost of the 1873 City Hall and Market House to $470,000.[82]

In order to finance the building's price tag, which was almost double the original estimate, the City Council increased Houston's city limits. One historian who was no fan of Mayor Scanlan wrote, "[A]t a stroke of the pen, the area of Houston was increased from nine square miles to twenty-five square miles and bonds were issued against the entire territory."[83]

As the new building took shape, Houstonians turned their attention to the November 1872 general election. For the first time in six years, the new city charter allowed them to choose their own city officials, and for the first time in twelve years, they could choose presidential electors. Mayor Scanlan

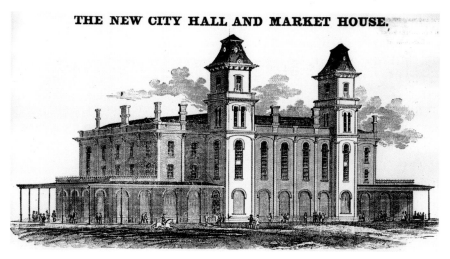

Houston's Second City Hall and Market House. Courtesy of Historic Houston Photographs, Special Collections, University of Houston Libraries.

was reelected, along with a board of Radical aldermen, while Houston Democrats rejoiced in the results of the statewide vote that gave their party a majority in the Texas legislature and elected Richard Coke as governor. For white southerners, a new day had dawned. For black Texans, November 1872 marked the beginning of oppressive laws that were designed to enforce a social and economic segregation that still persists.[84]

On December 19, 1872, a citizens' petition was submitted to City Council for the removal of City Engineer Charles Emerson Hoar, who "does not seem to suit the views of the petitioners." Hoar's contract as city engineer was not renewed in February 1873.[85]

When the three-story brick building opened in June 1873, it was described as "magnificent," but as difficulties arose over rental of the market space and as the theater and the roof began to leak, the complex was renamed "Our White Elephant."[86]

Between 1873 and 1874, the U.S. Congress passed an Amnesty Act that removed voting and office-holding restrictions on most former members of the Confederacy. At the state election in November 1873, Democrats swept Republicans out of office, and Richard Coke was reelected governor. Coke immediately removed Scanlan as Houston's mayor and replaced him with James Theodore Dudley Wilson, Robert Wilson's eldest son. J.T.D. Wilson, a significant landowner who was active in the real estate business, completed his term as mayor in 1874. He was followed on January 1, 1875, by Irwin Capers "I.C." Lord, a machinist and co-owner of Richardson's Eagle Iron Works who served through 1876. Texans adopted their sixth Constitution on February 15, 1876, by a vote of 136,606 to 56,652. It is still the basic organic law of Texas.[87]

On July 8, 1876, a suspicious fire started on the stage of the Academy of Music. A city employee who tried to sound the alarm found the rope of the fire bell cut. A crowd of about twenty thousand people watched the building burn to the ground. To add insult to injury, four days after the fire, the supposedly fireproof vault that contained city documents was opened. Only ashes were found inside. After the fire, it was discovered that the complex had been insured for only $100,000. The insurance company refused to pay; instead, it oversaw the design and construction of the third City Hall and Market House at a cost to itself of no more than $100,000. In order to select a design that would fit within its budget, it sponsored a competition that was won by Galveston architect Edward J. Duhamel.[88]

Unlike Carl de Grote and Charles Emerson Hoar, Edward Duhamel (1830–1911) was a professional architect. In 1867, he had apprenticed with a Buffalo architect who put him in charge of the firm's office until 1875, when he moved to Galveston. He practiced architecture on his own account in Houston, Galveston, and Austin before moving his family and business to Houston after winning the design contest. The Britton & Long Company began the construction of Houston's third City Hall over the foundation of the destroyed building in October 1876. Luckily, the three-thousand-pound fire bell from the first City Hall had been salvaged and hung in a makeshift tower on Market Square, while a temporary wood-frame shed again housed the municipal market.[89]

On November 9, 1877, the *Galveston Daily News* reported, "This new structure, whose building has been very tedious, will probably be turned over to the city next week. The new floor is nearly complete, and the various halls and offices in the second story ready for occupation. It is, in many respects, a superior edifice to the one destroyed by fire in 1876."[90] The "new" citizens of the enlarged Houston were stuck with helping to pay the $470,000 debt on the old building.

HOUSTON'S THIRD CITY HALL, 1877–1904

James Theodore Dudley Wilson served a second term as mayor between 1877 and 1878. After "a two years rest…[he had been] persuaded by the citizens to try his hand again. This was literally true for at that time a man had to be persuaded to take such an onerous office as that of the debt-burdened city."[91]

Duhamel's City Hall was completed in 1878 within the insurance company's budget. Critics said that, while the Italianate exterior was similar to but "more sophisticated" than that of the 1873 structure, it "did not have its predecessor's interior elegance." The one-story market pavilions on each side of the central block became two-story structures. "The detailing, crested roof, and chimneys remained, while subtle changes, such as the shape of the arched apertures, gave the newer city hall a distinctive appearance." The 100-foot-by-125-foot three-story central block was bordered by two asymmetrical corner towers. A new clock featured faces that looked north, east, south, and west from the taller south tower. A "kind of" new 2,800-pound bell cast by the Fulton Bell Company of Pittsburgh, Pennsylvania, was barely visible in the north tower. The old, 3,000-pound fire bell from the first and second City Halls, which was "rendered unfit for service" after the 1876 fire, had been shipped to Pittsburgh, where it was reused in casting the new, "finer-toned bell" bearing the inscription: "Cast by A. Fulton's Son & Co., Pittsburgh, Pa., A.D. 1876—Houston City Fire Department, Texas."[92]

Houston's *City Directory, 1877–1878*, listed the City Council as meeting at City Hall again every Friday at 4:00 p.m. A.J. Burke, Houston's mayor for the year 1879, told his City Council, "We commence the new administration under embarrassing circumstances…burthened with a heavy debt."[93] The next mayor, William R. Baker, a successful businessman, served for six years. Dr. S.O. Young wrote that, during this time, Baker and other leaders decided to apply "business methods" to solving the city's bond obligations. Their bondholders, "knowing that such important men could not afford to be mixed up in anything such as repudiating a debt…became firm and insistent."[94]

Houston had changed significantly in the fifty years since Baker had traveled from Baldwinsville, New York, in 1837 to help the Allen and Baldwin families establish their new Texas town. "During the 1880s, Houston gained 11,000 new residents, an increase that boosted its population to 27,600

Houston's Third City Hall and Market House. Courtesy of Historic Houston Photographs, Special Collections, University of Houston Libraries.

people." Many of these new Houstonians were highly skilled, relatively well-paid blue-collar employees of the railroads that traveled through Houston or of all those railroads' supporting industries. The city also boasted of "young professionals," including "a new breed of lawyers, corporate executives, and nascent entrepreneurs." These young men were represented by two new organizations, the Knights of Labor and the Young Men's Democratic Club, which banded together to help elect mechanical engineer Daniel Cargill Smith (1836–1915) as Houston's mayor in 1886.[95]

When Smith took office, the "city's finances were in deplorable condition," but just like "plastics" were the wave of the future in the 1950s, "fees" were economic magic in the 1880s. Public utilities enabled Houston and its citizens to move from the past into the future, paying the city "franchise fees" in exchange for access to public property. In 1888 alone, the gas company operated twenty miles of mains, the Houston Street Railway Company had six streetcar lines with fourteen miles of track, and the telephone company had 265 subscribers. In addition, developers paid the city fees as part of the $1,000,000 they invested in new buildings that year.[96]

When the mayor was able to pay interest on municipal bonds without emptying the treasury, the bondholders agreed on a compromise that permitted the city to make needed improvements—more public utilities, more sewers and paved streets, and more brick buildings—and "pay interest regularly on the reduced debt." Under a new city charter granted by the state legislature in 1889, "all municipal debts were finally settled. Relieved at last of its onerous fiscal burdens, Houston faced a new era."[97]

On July 15, 1890, the day after her eighty-fifth birthday, the *Houston Daily Post* referred to Charlotte Marie Baldwin Allen, the widow of Augustus Chapman Allen, as the "connecting link between Houston's past and present history." Several years later, it was discovered that the Allens' deed, which had donated Block 34 to the City of Houston in 1854, had never been filed in the Harris County Deed Records. In fact, the original deed was lost. On January 12, 1895, Mrs. Allen graciously deeded Block 34 to the city a second time. When Mrs. Allen died shortly afterward on August 3, 1895, flags in the city she had helped found flew at half-staff, and the day of her funeral was declared a day of mourning.[98]

In February 1901, workers began to repair the damage City Hall had suffered during the great hurricane of September 1900. The following June, Houston's third City Hall and Market House burned to the ground. Pressure was so low in the city's outdated water system that water from the firefighters' hoses could not reach the building's roof. Although the

Grave of and Monument to Charlotte Marie Baldwin Allen (1805–1895), Glenwood Cemetery, 2120 Washington Road. Photograph courtesy of Sandra Lord.

municipal records that were hurriedly stuffed into the vault were saved, the city departments again moved into temporary space. The Milby & Dow Building, which was located at 611 Travis Street, became Houston's "municipal headquarters."[99]

Houston's Fourth City Hall, 1904–1939

When the twentieth century arrived, many Houstonians believed that their City Hall and public market should be separated. City officials agreed, but even though they had obtained a quitclaim deed for Block 34, they decided that their new building would, as before, combine city government offices with the city market.[100]

The project's architect, George Edwin Dickey (1840–1910), had moved to Houston in 1878 to design the Capitol Hotel (1883–1911) on the site of today's Rice Lofts (1913) at 909 Texas Avenue and Main Street. Dickey left Houston in 1897 to practice in New Orleans but returned to design the

1904 City Hall and marketplace. Of the numerous public, commercial, and residential buildings Dickey designed during his years in Houston, only the Sweeney, Coombs, and Fredericks Building (1889) at 301 Main Street has survived.[101]

Houston contractor Alfred Thomas Lucas (1862–1922) began working on Houston's fourth City Hall and marketplace in November 1902. The new building rose "from the ruins that have so long lent the air of hideousness to the busiest square within the limits of the municipality," opening on December 30, 1903, at a cost below $100,000.[102] One historian considered the complex "in every way superior to" the previous city halls and marketplaces. "The building is an imposing structure," he wrote, "and with its two lofty towers has become a familiar landmark of Houston….[I]t is not only a beautiful building but it is a very useful and convenient one."[103]

The first floor's exterior was dominated by rough gray ashlar stone arches. The entrance facing Travis Street was in the middle of a three-story center block between two towers. It terminated in a central pediment with an ornamental carved stone at its apex that bore the date 1903. The second and third stories were constructed of buff bricks with ornamental stone trim. Numerous gables broke the lines of the slate-covered, steep-pitched roof. The interior of the building was finished in natural pine and boasted of steam heat, electric lights, modern plumbing, and telephones.[104] The ground floor housed the marketplace, while government offices were located on the second and third floors. The large council chamber faced Travis Street on the Preston Avenue end of the building. Its walls were lined with pictures of "as many of the mayors of Houston as it was possible to get."[105]

Like Duhamel's two towers, Dickey's were asymmetrical. The taller tower on the south side of the building held a massive new Seth Thomas chime clock with four glass faces, each 7.5 feet in diameter. Benajah Harvey Carroll wrote, "The bell that strikes the hours and half hours, was cast for the city in 1876, has passed through two fires and consequently has sounded its own downfall on two occasions, and is still as serviceable as when it was placed in the first tower." Rising from the pinnacle of the south tower were a weathervane and direction marker.[106] A new eight-hundred-pound fire alarm bell, which was connected to the city's fire alarm system, was in the north tower.

This tale of clocks and bells was confirmed in 1948 by first assistant city attorney Will Sears, who had studied the history of Houston's city halls. He told the *Houston Chronicle*, "In the old days, the clock had a bell that struck the hour. [Another] bell, Mr. Sears recalled, was tolled during funerals of prominent Houstonians and was rung to give notice of fires."[107]

Houston's Fourth City Hall and Market House. Courtesy of Historic Houston Photographs, Special Collections, University of Houston Libraries.

On St. Patrick's Day in 1905, Houston's first public monument, a Carrara marble statue of Confederate hero Richard "Dick" Dowling (1838–1867), sculpted by Frank A. Teich, was unveiled in front of Houston's 1904 City Hall. It sat on the south side of the building's large lawn until 1939. Later, an ornamental fountain was installed on the north side of the lawn.[108]

In 1914, the cornerstone was laid for a City Hall Annex with two stories and a basement. Architects Sanguinet, Staats, and Gottlieb and City Architect Maurice J. Sullivan positioned the neoclassical structure across the rear of Dickey's building. It was faced in Bedford limestone with terra cotta trim and stretched from Congress Street on the north to Preston Street on the south and out to the edge of the sidewalk on Milam Street on the west. Often referred to as "City Hall," the building housed Houston's principal city offices, including the traffic court on the first floor, and was open from 7:00 a.m. through 9:00 p.m. during the work week.[109]

On April 21, 1920, a "Cenotaph to the Unknown Soldier" was erected in front of City Hall, commemorating the two hundred Harris County men who had died in World War I.[110] Screens hid the front of the market stalls, and flowers and shrubs were planted around the building. By then, significant changes had occurred in Houston. Horses and carriages had been replaced by automobiles, trucks, and buses; residential areas had become commercial centers; and undeveloped land, farms, ranches, and plantations were Houston's new residential neighborhoods. As the city's prime retail shopping district shifted south on Main Street, past Texas Avenue, Market Square became a lower-income shopping district. The same was not true of the "farmer's market." As Houston's population grew, Market Square became so badly congested that, in 1924, "farmers and housewives clamored for more suitable accommodations."[111]

Three years later, Houstonians approved a $1,000,000 bond issue for a new city hall. While disagreement about the location of this newer and more modern seat of local government stalled any decision, the city finally did acquiesce to shoppers' demands and open a new farmer's market on March 21, 1929, on land that bordered Buffalo Bayou between Texas Avenue and Preston Street. Eighteen months later, thirty thousand purchasers bought 603 truckloads of produce valued at approximately $20,000, a number that increased to $500,000 the next year. By 1941, a widespread increase in vegetable and fruit production in Harris County established Houston as a produce center.[112]

Through a straw vote in November 1934, Houstonians indicated their preference for the site of a new City Hall—city land near Hermann Square Park surrounded by Smith and Bagby Streets and McKinney and Walker Streets. On December 3, 1939, Houston's city government moved into its fifth, and current, City Hall, which is located at 901 Bagby Street in an area unofficially known as the "civic center."[113] The first definitive plan for a civic center emerged from the city planning commission in 1926, as it debated over what to do with the new Hermann Square Park and Spanish Renaissance–style Houston Public Library. City Council consistently rejected creating a government-owned civic center because of its cost; too much of the needed land was in private hands.

Finally, in 1958, the city set aside $4,000,000 in bond funding to acquire forty separate tracts of land and create the Oscar Holcombe Civic Center. City Hall (1939), the Houston Public Library (1927), Hermann Square Park (1939), and the Sam Houston Coliseum and Music Hall (1937) eventually joined the Jesse H. Jones Hall for the Performing Arts (1966), the Albert Thomas Convention Center (1967, today's Bayou Place), and the Civic Center Garage, which sits under Lynn Wyatt Plaza (1967) and stretches

Paul Hester, "Photo Reference Number 23, Aerial View, 1980," National Register of Historic Places Inventory—Nomination Form, Main Street/ Market Square Historic District, 83004471.

all the way to Tranquillity Park (1979). In August 1989, not long after the Gus S. Wortham Theater Center (1987) and Sesquicentennial Park (1989 and 1998, respectively) replaced the farmer's market, the civic center was renamed the Theater District. In 2011, the Theater District became part of Houston First Corporation, which operates Houston's publicly owned hotel, performing arts, and convention facilities.[114]

Now What? 1939–1961

As 1940 dawned, the area around Block 34 was a ghost town except for the Bowen Bus Center, the new name for the 1904 City Hall building. It was open to the public around the clock, seven days a week, offering, in addition to transit operations, a coffee shop, a cigar stand, a buffet, and a tailor shop.[115]

On May 4, 1940, Thomas Pierce Converse, the grandson and sole heir of Augustus and Charlotte Allen, threatened to file suit to regain title to Block 34. He estimated the land was worth $1,000,000. City attorney Sewall Myers responded, "The city legal department has found that the city has outright title and can use the property for any purpose it sees fit."[116] Before the city won the lawsuit, Converse was murdered.

Charlotte and Augustus Allen had four children, only one of whom, Martha Elizabeth (1838–1886), nicknamed "Eliza," survived to maturity. On April 19, 1859, Eliza married Frank B. Chase, a conductor on the Houston and Texas Central Railway. Sadly, Mr. Chase died seven months later. On September 21, 1863, Eliza married Colonel James Converse (1828–1900), the general superintendent of the Galveston, Harrisburg and San Antonio Railway, the successor company to the 1850 Buffalo Bayou, Brazos and Colorado Railway. Eliza died in San Antonio in 1886, nine years before her mother, leaving behind one ten-year-old son, Thomas Pierce Converse (1876–1943).

On July 18, 1943, exactly 105 years after Eliza's birth, Thomas's third wife, Myrtle, discovered her husband writing a letter to another woman. The couple argued, and later that night, Thomas attacked Myrtle with a ten-inch steel chisel. Myrtle's son, a thirty-one-year-old cab driver, warned Thomas to stop. When Thomas persisted, the young man shot him once in the back with a .38-caliber pistol, but he said, "He kept going after her, so I just kept firing the pistol. When I saw him fall, I called the police and an ambulance."[117] After Thomas's murder, Myrtle and her attorney, W.F. Watts, whom she later married, took Converse's place as plaintiffs to the suit and lost.[118]

Dickey's building survived intact until a two-alarm fire in April 1946 damaged the south tower. Two years later, the tops of the unstable towers were removed. Leaking in the two towers had rotted the floors, and the mortar around the tower wall bricks had deteriorated until the bricks could be pushed out by hand. The 1903 Seth Thomas clock and the 1876 bell were stored in the basement of the 1904 building.[119]

Houston's population reached the one million mark on July 4, 1954, thanks to air conditioning and a booming economy.[120] Between 1960 and 1980, Houston grew from the seventh-largest city in the United States to the fifth-largest.[121] Joining the national trend away from the "old" toward "urban renewal" in the 1950s and 1960s, property owners around Market Square demolished historic buildings, cleared land, and installed garages and surface parking lots for the businesspeople who drove into downtown during the work week.[122] The 1904 building ceased being a bus terminal in the spring of 1960, shortly before burning down in a five-alarm fire on the night of Sunday, May 22, 1960. After the fire was put out, the 1903 Seth Thomas Clock was crated up and moved to a space beneath the parking ramp between the City Hall Annex and the Sam Houston Coliseum.[123]

The 1876 bell seemed to have disappeared. It wasn't until Tuesday, May 24, 1960, as fire inspectors continued to probe the building's ruins, that they "discovered the huge bell in an undamaged basement section." Fire Chief C.M. Bullock "said it would be polished, restored to its original state, and mounted" in the city's Fire Alarm Building at 1010 Bagby Street.[124] In a later story in the *Houston Chronicle*, District Chief W.C. Simonton said that he was one of the fire inspectors who found the clock as the "wrecking crew was about to haul it away for junk." He reported that the clock had remained fire department property and that, while the original plan was for it to "be mounted in the fire alarm building on Bagby, that plan never materialized. The tentative plan in 1967 was that the bell would be given a place of honor in the new Fire Station No. 1 on Preston." Until then, the bell would remain "in the care of Simonton at the present No. 1 station at 403 Caroline."[125]

Peter Boesel, "Photo Reference Number 1, Market Square, 1982," National Register of Historic Places Inventory—Nomination Form, Main Street/Market Square Historic District, 83004471.

As the charred remains of the 1904 City Hall were being demolished in August and September 1960, the owner of the demolition company remarked, "[I]t was a strong building, with walls seven bricks thick in some places." He estimated that it contained 450,000 "pink, hand-made bricks."[126] The City Hall Annex was demolished in the summer of 1963.[127]

In the interim, the mayor and City Council debated how Block 34 could again contribute to the city's revenue stream. One of the ideas batted about in 1961 included leasing the block to the Old Market Corp. for $2,500 a month, with an option to buy it for $524,947. The corporation planned to build a multistory motel garage on the site. When the idea became an ordinance, the Old Market Square Association, a volunteer organization dedicated to creating a "real park," obtained eight thousand signatures opposing the city's plan and forced a special referendum election on the issue. Their contention was that the sale was a bad business deal for the city. They advocated instead for a landscaped park with underground parking. The citizens prevailed, and on July 26, 1961, Block 34 became Market Square Park.[128]

MARKET SQUARE PARK, 1961–2020

For fifteen years, history disappeared under waves of construction and nightlife took off and then cratered while the city stalled in delivering the landscaped park they had promised, and Houstonians who supported preservation struggled to attract the public's attention.

In the beginning, the area around Market Square Park was *the* place to be. "[S]ome of the oldest buildings in Houston, including many that were out of use, were converted into *boîtes de luxe* for the 'boldfaced types,' as the *Chronicle*'s Big City Beat columnist Maxine Mesinger styled them." The Old Market Square Association published the *Market Square Gazette*, advertising "underground" shops and weekend art sales on the sidewalks surrounding the park for the tourists and folks from the suburbs who loved strolling past the area's old buildings. By the early 1970s, however, Old Market Square had already seen its heyday. Former nightclubs were converting to strip clubs and peep shows, as the demolition of historic buildings that began in the late 1960s continued, leaving the square (and the historic district) almost forgotten.[129]

In 1972, as One Shell Plaza topped out at fifty stories, making Houston the "oil capital of the world," interviews with developers, political leaders, and civic boosters all seemed to echo the same refrain: "Houston looks to the future, not the past." Everyone wanted to live in Houston. It was new and exciting—the sixth-largest city in the United States—but it had no center, no beating heart.[130]

On May 20, 1976, a glimmer of hope appeared as the Junior League of Houston's Bicentennial Committee presented $60,000 in seed money to the City of Houston for landscaping Market Square Park. The winning design by B.F. Rodriguez-Castinado, an associate of Fred Buxton and Associates, was to be a park "where the people [could] find comfort and a place to rest and enjoy nature." A new tower for the 1903 Seth Thomas Clock and the 1876 bell "was the catalyst for the whole plan."[131]

The Houston Chamber of Commerce's bicentennial gift was Tranquillity Park, a roof garden over an extension of the civic center's underground parking garage. As earth was removed from Tranquillity Park, it was trucked north to Market Square Park, where it was massaged into undulating "hills," joining trees from an anonymous donor and benches already installed by the city. A Texas Historical Commission Marker for "Old Market Square" was installed on Milam Street, near Congress Street. By 1977, the completed park was restful, but because of the "hills" and erratic lighting and policing, it never became the popular gathering space its designer and supporters had envisioned, nor did it include a new tower for the 1903 clock and the 1876 bell.[132]

Since it was discovered in 1960, the bell had been in the safekeeping of the Houston Fire Department. The clock was packed in crates and safely stored beneath the parking ramp that connected the City Hall Annex and the Sam Houston Coliseum. In August 1968, there was a gas line explosion beneath the parking ramp where the clock was stored. The clock was not harmed, but it needed a new home. The city agreed to lease the clock for one dollar per year for ten years to the Old Market Square Association, which moved it, still in crates, to the basement of the M&M Building (today, the University of Houston–Downtown). Ten years later, Houston's parks director announced plans to construct a new tower to house the clock, despite the fact that only one hundred dollars had been raised for the project. When someone went to check on the crates that contained the 1903 clock parts, they were nowhere to be found.[133]

A while later, A. Pat Daniels, a longtime Houston history buff and then-publisher of the *Market Square Gazette*, read an article about the Heritage Garden Village in Woodville, Texas. A photograph with the article showed a building with a large clock. Daniels did some research and confirmed, as he had suspected, that the clock in Woodville was the 1903 Seth Thomas Clock from Houston.

The owner of Heritage Garden Village was an artist by the name of Clyde Gray.[134] Daniels and his fellow preservationists petitioned City Council about the clock until the legal department sued Mr. Gray in 1979. Mr. Gray reported that someone in Houston had sold the clock to an antique dealer in 1974. The clock had passed through several hands before Gray discovered it lying in an open field that belonged to a junk dealer in Shepherd, Texas. Gray purchased the clock for less than $1,000 and had it shipped to Woodville. He researched the records of the Seth Thomas Clock Co. of Thomaston, Connecticut, and confirmed that he was in possession of the 1903 clock that had adorned Houston's City Hall. Gray then spent several months and several thousand dollars working with an expert to put the clock back in working condition for his exhibit. He told the attorneys from Houston's legal department that he figured he had obtained the clock fairly and refused to return it.[135]

The subsequent lawsuit confirmed that the City of Houston had retained title to the clock, despite its travels from the M&M Building to Woodville, Texas. Gray said he had no objection to returning the clock to Houston if and when the city could provide a suitable home. The Council "paid tribute to Gray's efforts to preserve the clock by making him an honorary Houstonian" and by approving an agreement with Gray by which the city leased the clock to him for ten years (1979–1989) in exchange for one dollar. The city maintained the option of claiming the clock after five years (1984) if it obtained "a suitable display area." Mr. Gray went back to Woodville and continued to take care of the clock at his own expense.[136]

Although Houston's Main Street Market Square Historic District was listed in the National Register of Historic Places in 1983, many of its business owners "felt the city did little to embrace and promote the area.…In a 1984 *Houston Post* essay, Charles Segers, then a writer and editor for Prudential Insurance, said of the area in general, 'Old Market Square was like Bourbon Street, except that it had an atmosphere of the forbidden that I had never experienced on Bourbon Street.' The Houston establishment never really approved of what was going on down at Market Square, despite the tourist dollars it was bringing in."[137]

In 1982, Jim Barlow of the *Houston Chronicle* wrote, "The clock which graced the old City Hall in downtown Houston may be coming home to Market Square by the beginning of 1984. The city of Houston, the Downtown Houston Association, and the Junior League have plans to bring the huge old clock back to Market Square along with a revamping of the block-

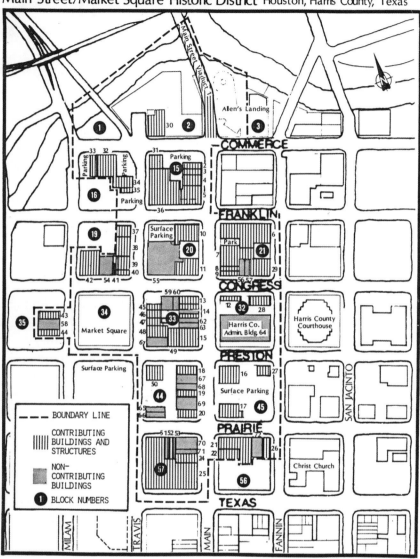

Map of Main Street/Market Square Historic District, 1983, National Register of Historic Places Inventory—Nomination Form, Main Street/Market Square Historic District, 83004471.

square park itself." Those plans were opposed by the Old Market Square Preservation Committee and a new group, the Committee to Liberate Our Clock Kwickly (CLOCK), which wanted to return the clock to its rightful place but did not agree with the redesign.[138]

A preliminary plan for the park called for a concrete amphitheater with grass terraces in front of a stage on one corner, a small pond in the center, and the new clock tower on another corner. The new tower would incorporate the original plans for the 1904 clock tower, which had been located by the Downtown Houston Association. The Old Market Square Preservation Committee felt that the proposed design would only intensify the problems caused by the hills engineered into the 1977 park. The organization wrote in a letter to City Council, "Those residents of Houston who have been in the area at times other than during special events know that the habitués of the park primarily are drifters and drunks.…The park is rarely used by those who would like to rest on the benches or on the greenery of the park or enjoy sack lunches because of the fear of being mugged, insulted or otherwise offended."[139]

Initiated by DiverseWorks Inc. in 1985, the Market Square Project was a separate nonprofit, tax-exempt organization formed by the City of Houston Parks and Recreation Department, DiverseWorks, the Downtown Houston Association, and five artists. Gerald D. Hines Interests provided project management on a pro bono basis, and SWA provided architectural services.[140] In 1986, the Municipal Arts Commission approved the five artists selected by a panel process to create the works that would be "planted" in the redesigned Market Square Park: James Surls, Richard Turner, Doug Hollis, Paul Hester, and Malou Flato. While each artist created a signature piece, the five worked together as a team, which resulted in the park becoming "a work of art in itself."[141]

Phase I, site preparation, was completed in 1987. In Phase II, the Houston Market Square Park Project Inc., a new nonprofit corporation formed in 1988, funded and built out the artists' design.[142] In 1988, Clyde Gray sold his museum complex to the Tyler County Heritage Society, which asked Houston to take the clock back. The Houston Parks and Recreation Department retrieved the clock and stored its many crates in their warehouse.[143] In August 1990, the 1903 clock finally came out of storage and was displayed at the Heritage Society's Museum of Texas History in Sam Houston Park as part of a Classic American Clocks exhibit.[144] In the same year, Houston's City Council designated the Main Street Market Square Historic District the city's first Historic District.

The following year, the Main Street Market Square Historic District was accepted into the Texas Historical Commission's new Texas Main Street Program, which assisted in the economic revitalization of business districts and the preservation of historic downtown structures. Funded by a Community Development Block Grant from the city, the Greater Houston Preservation Alliance (now Preservation Houston), and the Downtown Houston Association, the Market Square Historic District Project evolved into the Downtown Historic District Inc. in 1995. It implemented a façade grant program, made a $25,000 donation to the Friedman Clock Tower Project, organized special events to promote the area, and formed a committee to promote business in clubs and restaurants. "These efforts helped fuel millions of investment dollars in new residential, restaurant, and entertainment businesses and the renovation of over 30 buildings."[145]

When the group led by Daniels again insisted that the clock be placed in its original location in Market Square Park, the park's planners responded that because the clock wasn't located until after the design work was finished, there was no longer a place for it.[146]

The third Market Square Park was dedicated on June 25, 1992. Austin artist Malou Flato created four pairs of curving benches, which she inlaid with hand-painted tiles suggesting scenes from Market Square's past. Each pair of benches was located next to the sidewalk of the four streets surrounding the park. Eighty photographs from Houston's past and present were selected by Paul Hester, who permanently etched them on enamel tiles that were inlaid in the park's benches, creating "a scrapbook or photo album of the city." Four diagonal crosswalks extended from each corner of the tree-studded, grass-covered square into a central plaza. Artists Doug Hollis and Richard Turner embedded masonry fragments from demolished local structures and recycled bricks in the crosswalks. The central plaza was "sized to accommodate approximately 150 people" and featured James Surls's twenty-five-foot-high, painted steel and wood sculpture, *Points of View.*[147]

In 1994, Houston businessman Kenneth Meyer donated a twenty-foot-by-twenty-foot plot of land that he owned at the southeast corner of Congress and Travis Streets to the city to be used as a public park featuring a clock tower. Architect Barry Moore and the Mathes Group designed the tower and its park setting. Meyer and the members of the Clock Tower Project raised the funds to build the tower. In 1995, Saul and Elaine Friedman donated the funds that were needed to begin building the sixty-five-foot tower named in honor of Mr. Friedman's parents, Louis and Annie Friedman, who were immigrants from Hungary and Russia. A large marker at the base of the

James Surls, "Points of View," Market Square Park, 1991. Photograph courtesy of Sandra Lord.

tower tells the story of Saul Friedman's parents' "ambitions and achievements and the opportunities afforded them by the American dream." On May 10, 1996, the four-faced 1903 Seth Thomas Clock and the 1876 bell from the south tower of Houston's 1904 City Hall were reunited in Houston's tiniest park.[148] The inner workings of the clock are visible at street level; the cost to the city was ten dollars, plus the expense of restoring the clock.

The third design of Market Square Park had many of the same problems as the first two. On some days, there was virtually no life in the square except for homeless people who were looking for a place to sleep and dog-walkers who were heading for one of the only places in downtown Houston with a large grassy area. The City of Houston was well aware of the problem. "Although Market Square is often touted as the most promising starting point for rejuvenating downtown, significant new development in the area has so far been elusive." In an effort to make the area "more attractive for development," City Council created Houston's third Tax Increment Reinvestment Zone in December 1995 in order to finance improvements in the historic neighborhood over the next thirty years.[149]

Despite City Council making property buyers and owners in the Historic District eligible for tax breaks in March 1997, thus encouraging the preservation of historically significant property in the area, other priorities came before redesigning Market Square Park. Redevelopment of the 1913 Rice Hotel into the cutting-edge Post Rice Lofts in 1998 was considered the linchpin for downtown's renaissance. The Cotswold Project (1995–2006) involved a total remake of downtown's ninety-block historic center. Landscaping, new streetlights, fountains, and improved parking were installed in order to make downtown streets more pedestrian-friendly.[150] Work on the redesign of Market Square Park started in July 1997, "financed by $725,000 in donated funds and $50,000 in federal and city funds." The project was "expected to take six months"—it took ten years.[151]

The City of Houston Parks and Recreation Department, the Downtown Redevelopment Authority, and the Houston Downtown Management District formed a collaboration determined to eliminate the negative perception of Market Square Park and bring it back to life.[152] They contracted with the Project for Public Spaces (PPS) to come to Houston, study the park, and reach out to the community. Following the example of PPS, the team that designed and planned the fourth Market Square Park—Lauren Griffith Associates, a Houston-based landscape architect; architect Kerry Goelzer; and Ray + Hollington Architects—spent time between 2007 and 2008 listening to the desires and concerns voiced by residents, businesses, and visitors.[153] Their

Friedman Clock Tower, 2019. Photograph courtesy of Linda Pham.

plan met all of the primary goals set for the redesigned park: to acknowledge the history of the site; to provide an active, urban green space adapted to the needs of a diverse neighborhood; and to conserve its existing artwork while incorporating new works of art.[154]

Tribble & Stephens began construction in December 2009. The park was regraded to create sightlines from surrounding sidewalks for visibility and safety, all of the existing trees were preserved, and energy-efficient lighting was installed to create a mellow ambience at night, keeping the urban park safe.[155] On August 28, 2010, the fourth Market Square Park opened. It has been a resounding success since day one. It is well-lit, well-maintained, and well-policed; most importantly, it has helped stimulate economic development in the Historic District while preserving the past.

Through an interlocal agreement, the Houston Downtown Management District operates and programs Market Square Park on behalf of the City of Houston. The park is open from 6:00 a.m. to 11:00 p.m. daily. Information

Barbara, Marie, Lorie, and Wendy, April 2011. Photograph courtesy of Sandra Lord.

about scheduled events in Market Square Park can be found at www. MarketSquarePark.com.

There are two concrete columns at the corner of Travis and Congress Streets near the park's BCycle station.[156] The "gargoyle" column has a panel with Park Site Chronology, while the other column features some of Paul Hester's 1991 etchings of historic photographs. As a reminder of the old City Hall Market House, you'll find a kiosk on the north side of the park

Richard Turner, History Walk, Market Square Park, 2019. Photograph courtesy of Sandra Lord.

with a walk-up window where you can order food and beverages daily. Restrooms are located on the Milam Street side of the kiosk. South of the kiosk, you can spread a blanket on the grassy central lawn surrounded by mature live oaks or sit on a chair in the plaza facing Travis Street in front of a trellis shaded by Mexican sycamores. The trellis also functions as a small stage for performances and gatherings. James Surls's 1991 sculpture *Points of View* was moved from the center to the south side of the park, just beyond the plaza and trellis. It is surrounded by a gentle water feature.

Austin artist Malou Flato's four two-sided benches pair off on each side of the park. Flato attributed their curving design to James Surls. "He kept talking about circles," she said. She broke frost-proof porcelain tiles into chips then hand placed them to create impressionistic scenes from the old Market Square. The benches facing Travis Street feature people shopping for trinkets at the Market House. On the south side of the park, facing Preston Street, the mosaic-tile benches and a matching "watertable" fountain are decorated with straw hats similar to those worn during hot southern summers at the turn of the twentieth century.[157]

As you stroll through the west side of the park, following Richard Turner's repurposed architectural fragments from 1991 embedded in a "history walk," look for a long black granite band in the ground running parallel to Travis Street. It indicates the back wall of the last three City Halls. They all faced Travis Street and featured a northern tower, where the kiosk is located, and a southern tower, where the Surls sculpture is located. If you don't feel alone, even when there's no one else in the park, it's because you are standing with thousands of "ghosts."

The dual metal skyline on top of a fence near the corner of Preston and Milam Streets was designed by Paul Hester and was crafted and installed by

Richard Turner, History Walk, Market Square Park, 2019. Photograph courtesy of Sandra Lord.

Malou Flato, "Mosaic Tile Bench," Preston Street, Market Square Park, 2019. Photograph courtesy of Sandra Lord.

Blumenthal Sheet Metal in August 2010. Hester created an "old" Houston skyline along Buffalo Bayou facing the interior of the park. On the side facing out onto Milam Street, he highlighted Houston's 2010 skyline.

Malou Flato's third pair of mosaic-tile benches celebrates the colorful vegetables that were once available at the City Market House. It is positioned between two dog runs facing Milam Street, one for small dogs and one for large dogs. They are enclosed by a beautifully designed and lit crescent walkway, where everyone can enjoy watching the four-legged friends frolic. Water features are inside both runs, as are benches and canine drinking fountains. The Market Square Park dog runs were officially dedicated on May 21, 2011, by Mayor Annise Parker in memory of Houstonian Holly Anawaty. It was hard to decide which Holly loved more, her canine children, Bessie and Pete, or the children she helped during her many years as a social worker in Houston. Holly lost her battle with brain cancer in August 2006.

Flato's mosaic-tile benches facing Congress Street curve around a "watertable" fountain similar to the one on Preston Street. Behind the benches is Lauren's Garden, where delightful flowing water, beautiful

Malou Flato, "Mosaic Tile Bench," Milam Street, Market Square Park, 2019. Photograph courtesy of Sandra Lord.

Lauren's Garden, Market Square Park, 2019. Photograph courtesy of Sandra Lord.

sculpture, and seasonal flowers are dedicated to the victims of the attacks of September 11, 2001.

> [The garden] *was funded in memory of Lauren Catuzzi Grandcolas, a native Houstonian and the only Texan on United Flight 93. Three low, black granite walls with falling water represent the three crash sites: New York, Pennsylvania, and Washington, D.C. Each smooth stone in the fountain symbolizes a life lost. Water flows over a textured black plane around 40 stones for those who died on United Flight 93 and falls into a trough lined with 2,752 small stones for those who died at the World Trade Center, and 184 larger stones for those who died at the Pentagon....Ketria Bastien Scott's bronze sculptures of bristlecone pines, an organism that can survive 5,000 years, symbolize endurance.*[158]

Park plantings are designed to bloom sequentially year-round with colors that complement the Flato benches. Some plantings scent the garden; others attract butterflies and dragonflies hovering over the water. The yellow Forty

Paul Hester, "Houston Skyline," Market Square Park, 2010. Photograph courtesy of Sandra Lord.

Heroes Roses were bred in memory of Lauren and her fellow victims on Flight 93.[159] Sharon Connally Ammann's bronze bust of Lauren is nestled beneath Crape Myrtles; it was donated to the park by the Catuzzi family.

It would have been impossible to imagine in 1961, as Market Square lost its last remaining artifacts—the 1876 bell and the 1903 clock—that Block 34 would ever again be the vibrant center of Houston's Historic District. But this is Houston, where "The difficult is done immediately. The impossible may take a little longer."[160]

2

THE GHOSTS AROUND MARKET SQUARE PARK

THE PRESIDENT'S MANSION

*If one believed all the stories and traditions connected with President Sam
Houston, one would be forced to believe that he was ubiquitous…for there
are several places pointed out as "Sam Houston's home" in Houston.…Each
one of these stories may be true, but the fact remains that the official home of
the President of the Republic of Texas was in the President's mansion on the
southeast corner of Main and Preston* [Streets].[161]
—*B.H. Carroll,* Standard History of Houston

In 1836, Robert Wilson donated Block 43, south of Market Square, to
Sam Houston. Eventually, Houston donated or sold two lots on Block 43,
retaining ten lots for his family.[162] Beginning in May 1837, Houston, his
staff, and cabinet members officed in "the dog-trot on Travis," which had
been completed by Robert Boyce on Lots 9 and 10 of Block 43, facing
Travis Street. It was here that the President of the Republic of Texas met
John James Audubon (1785–1851) during the famous ornithologist's only
visit to Houston.[163]

*We landed at Houston, the capital of Texas, drenched to the skin, and
were kindly received on board the steamer* Yellow Stone [by] *Captain
West, who gave us his state-room to change our clothes, and furnished us*

400 Block of Caroline Street. Site of House where General Sam Houston lived, 1837–38. The marker was erected by the De Zavala Chapter, Texas Historical and Landmarks Association, 1928. Photograph courtesy of Sandra Lord.

refreshments and dinner.[164] *The Buffalo bayou had risen about six feet, and the neighboring prairies were partly covered with water; there was a wild and desolate look cast on the surrounding scenery....* [S]*hanties, cargoes of hogsheads, barrels, etc., were spread about the landing; and Indians drunk and hallooing were stumbling about in the mud in every direction....We walked towards the president's house, accompanied by the secretary of the navy, and as soon as we rose above the bank we saw before us a level of far-extending prairie, destitute of timber and of rather poor soil.*[165] *Houses, half finished, and most of them without roofs, tents and a liberty pole, with the capitol, were all exhibited to our view at once. We approached the president's mansion, however, wading through water above our ankles. This abode of President Houston is a small log house, consisting of two rooms, and a passage through, after the Southern fashion.*[166] *The moment we stepped over the threshold, on the right hand of the passage, we found ourselves ushered into what in other countries would be called the ante-chamber; the ground floor, however, was muddy and filthy, a large fire was burning, a small table covered with paper and writing materials was in the center, camp-beds, trunks and different materials were strewed around the room. We were at once presented to several members of the Cabinet....The president was engaged in the opposite room on national business, and we could not see him for some time. Meanwhile, we amused ourselves by walking to the capitol, which was yet without a roof, and the floors, benches, and tables of both houses of congress were as well saturated with water as our clothes had been in the morning....We first caught sight of President Houston as he walked from one of the grog-shops, where he had been to prevent the sale of ardent spirits. He was on his way to his house and wore a large coarse gray hat; he is upward of six feet high, and strong in proportion. But I observed a scowl in the expression of his eyes that was forbidding and disagreeable.*

We reached his abode before him, but he soon came, and we were presented to his excellency. He was dressed in a fancy velvet coat, and trowsers [sic] trimmed with broad gold lace; around his neck was tied a cravat somewhat in the style of seventy-six. He received us kindly, was desirous of retaining us for a while, and offered us every facility within his power. He at once removed us from the ante-room to his private chamber, which, by the way, was not much cleaner than the former....Our talk was short, but the impression which was made on my mind at the time by himself, his officers, and his place of abode, can never be forgotten.[167]

Not long after Audubon's visit, Charlotte Marie Baldwin Allen followed Augustus and John Allen to Houston and stayed in the log cabin that belonged to her brother-in-law, Henry Rowland Allen.[168] The day after her arrival in Houston:

[Sam Houston], *with his presidential household, accompanied Mrs. Allen horseback riding to what was then known as the Lamar Camp, three miles from the bayou.*[169] *The lateness of the hour threw them into the night, and for a time, the party was lost in the timber and had to remain there until General Houston himself went in search of a trail or camp and succeeded in discovering a light that led them to a place where they got directions to return to the log cabin and the camp of General Houston.*[170]

It wasn't long before Charlotte was able to move into the Allens' elegant new home in the 400 Block of Caroline Street between Preston and Prairie Streets (Lot 6, Block 48). According to their bookkeeper, William R. Baker, "The Allens threw open their own comfortable home, without charge, to all who needed lodgings in their town. Their...hospitality cost upward of $30,000 per year. But the Allens considered it an expense that would bring good returns in the development of their city."[171] Mary Austin Holley, Stephen F. Austin's cousin, had dinner on Christmas Day 1837 at the Allens' house, then stayed overnight as a guest. She wrote in her diary, "Staid [sic] all night with Mrs. Allen—very hospitably entertained—a new good house—well—even elegantly furnished."[172] Later, she wrote to her daughter that "he [Augustus Allen] is, of course, wealthy....She's a

"Sam Houston," Homer S. Thrall, A Pictorial History of Early Texas, St. Louis: N.D. Thompson & Co., 1879, 213. Courtesy of the Houston Metropolitan Research Center, Houston Public Library.

northern lady. They are very genteel people and live well. Have a good house and elegant furniture (mahogany, hair sofas, red velvet rocking chair, etc.) all nice and new, and in modern style."[173]

In the fall of 1837, Sam Houston moved into his "executive residence" next door to the Allens. It was a crude little house with two rooms and a lean-to that he shared with his friend, Ashbel Smith.[174] During her December 1837 visit to Houston, Mary Austin Holley wrote in her diary:

> *The President had not time to eat his dinner—seldom has. Lives next to Mrs. Allen's—his house has one room—always crowded with persons on business....The President's cabin has no glass—slats across the windows with blankets interwoven supply the place....*[You can] *hear the howling of wolves at night....When wearied past endurance he goes out & sits down on the prairie back of the cabin which makes his palace....A better house is building.*[175]

In February 1838, Houston himself described the log cabin on Caroline Street: "I am freezing in a miserable open house; four windows in it, and not one pane of glass nor shutter—three doors, and shutters to but two—no ceiling and the floor loose laid. Is not this a 'White House' with a plague to it?"[176]

After Francis Lubbock arrived in Houston on the *Laura* in January 1837, he "contracted for and had built a large wooden structure as a storehouse, costing nearly $6,000....Robert P. Boyce, was the builder."[177] The storehouse was located at the corner of Main and Preston Streets, the site of today's Scanlan Building at 405 Main Street. By September, Lubbock no longer needed the storehouse. He had chosen the security of a salary as assistant clerk of the House of Representatives over the insecurity of being self-employed as a merchant. A happy coincidence occurred that fall when, according to Lubbock:

> *The question of securing a residence at once for the president was proposed in congress, the friends of the measure urging the immediate necessity in consequence of his great discomfort. The government was about to issue a new currency. To the committee appointed to purchase a residence, I proposed to sell for $6,000 my store, a large old-time one-story house and a half story above, with dormer windows, if they would pay me for it out of the first money issued....During the next spring, congress voted $3,000 more for repairs; and* [after] *Lamar became President* [on December 10, 1838] *there was an additional appropriation of $5,000 to complete, repair, and furnish the executive mansion. As the capital was removed to Austin in the fall of 1839, President Lamar did not occupy this building long.*[178]

The move from his log cabin could not have come too soon for Sam Houston. In his February 1838 letter, he had also written, "The Palace is not yet finished, but it is said to be in progress and will soon be completed.

I have sent to New York for magnificent furniture, and when it arrives, what a beautiful contrast shall I enjoy!"[179] Houston asked master carpenter Robert Boyce, the builder of his dogtrot office on Block 43 and of Lubbock's storehouse, to submit an estimate of $6,000 for the "Palace." In his memoir, Boyce recalled that he refused, knowing that congress had appropriated only $3,000. When Houston insisted that he must have the new house for his personal comfort, Boyce again refused, saying that he would lose money. Finally, after Houston "suggested" that other government contracts would come Boyce's way to offset any loss on the White House, the carpenter gave in.[180]

To save money on his government contract, Boyce allowed his crew to sleep in the unfinished presidential house, where two brick fireplaces lessened the chill during the winter. President Houston suspected Boyce was delaying finishing the building in order to use it as a dormitory. After Houston repeated the accusation in front of a visiting English envoy, the carpenter called the president a "damned liar" and predicted that "he was headed for the 'bad place.'"[181]

Boyce finished the White House in early 1838, except for the panes of glass in a twelve-light sash. Colonel A.S. Thruston, the commissary general, accepted the dwelling for the republic withholding only $300 for the glass.[182] After President Houston moved in, he became dissatisfied with the style of the folding doors Boyce had installed between the two front reception rooms. He called Boyce in, and both men became angry. They called on Thruston to mediate their disagreement, and Boyce recalled, Thruston was forced to write his personal obligation to the government for the $2,700 he had already paid Boyce.[183]

In 1841, Houston wrote to his new wife, Margaret Lea Houston, that he had put the "Houston City house" up for sale. This was either the building on Block 43 or the one on Caroline Street.[184] Boyce took "personal revenge" in 1842, when both he and Houston applied for letters of administration in settling a mutual friend's estate. As administrator of the estate, Boyce refused to approve a $1,000 claim from Houston.[185]

In 1846 and 1850, after Texas became the twenty-eighth state in the United States, the federal government paid it "a substantial sum of money" in return for relinquishing its very tenuous claim to the upper Rio Grande, around Santa Fe, New Mexico.[186] Boyce, deciding that the time was propitious to collect his outstanding $300, made arrangements through their mutual friend, Francis Lubbock, to speak with now–United States Senator Houston in July 1852, after he had laid the cornerstone at the City of Houston's new Masonic temple.[187]

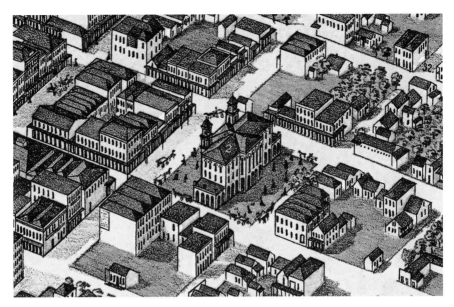

Houston, Texas, 1873. Bird's Eye View of the City of Houston, Texas 1873. Lithograph (hand-colored). Published by J.J. Stoner, Madison, Wisconsin, Center for American History, the University of Texas at Austin.

With hat in hand and "bowing profoundly," Boyce was at the head of the line to shake the great man's hand. "General," he said, "I am poor, and the money could be a great help to me." Houston recalled that his secretary, David P. Richardson, had been authorized to handle the contract and asked why Boyce had not approached him, all the time knowing that Richardson had died in August 1837.[188]

Next, Boyce applied to Thruston, who had moved to Kentucky, for the proper documentation, which he then presented to the state legislature. When that effort for relief also failed, Boyce approached Houston again in 1854.[189]

This time, the senator refused to shake Boyce's extended hand, saying that the builder had been exceedingly rude. Boyce contritely agreed but said that he had always supported Houston politically and added, "I have heard you say many times if a man cannot abuse his friends, who could he?" At this, Houston capitulated and agreed to endorse an order for the $300 if Boyce would write an apology for "his scandalous language." Boyce wrote triumphantly, "I got my money after all them years."[190]

IF THIS BLOCK COULD TALK[191]

All old citizens remember John Collins...the king of Houston retail grocers....He had a large two-story brick store at Travis Street and Preston Avenue...the best corner in the city, being on Preston Avenue, then the greatest business thoroughfare in Texas, for all the business done with the interior came over [the] Long Bridge at the foot of Preston, and also facing Market Square....In the late fifties Mr. Collins, a few weeks before Christmas, conceived the idea of cornering the turkey market. Next to his store was a vacant lot. He put up a rough board fence around it and put the turkeys in the enclosure. He bought all he could get hold of and a week before Christmas he had by actual count 400 turkeys....On the very night that he went to bed congratulating himself on the success of his scheme, some...bad boys cut the straps on his turkey pen gate and the next morning, the pen was empty. Every turkey there had departed for parts unknown. For a moment Mr. Collins was in despair, and then an inspiration seized him. He put out a board offering fifty cents for each of his turkeys returned to him. He had handbills scattered all over the city making the same offer. In an hour after the appearance of the handbills...all kinds of boys arrived with turkeys and by night the pen was pretty full again. The next day the turkey arrivals continued. Mr. Collins was kept busy paying out fifty-cent pieces. Then the pen got overcrowded, something that was not the case before, so Mr. Collins made an investigation and found on examination of his book that he had paid out $300 and that he had 200 turkeys more than he had before the boys cut the gate.... [T]he boys had scoured the city and county and brought in every turkey they could find.[192]

In 1866, all of the Preston Street side of Block 43 was occupied by grocers, including John Collins' shop on Lots 9 and 10 and Hardcastle & Co. on Lot 8. Block 43, like Market Square, is located in Houston's Fourth Ward, south of Congress Street and west of Main Street. The Fourth Ward has been called the "Mother Ward" because it was the area that first provided significant employment for African Americans who worked and lived in the city instead of on the surrounding farms and plantations. They loaded, unloaded, and transported goods that were entering and leaving Houston via roads, railroads, barges, and boats. After Juneteenth (June 19, 1865), African Americans were free to purchase land and establish homes in Houston.[193] Twenty-two freed slaves chose to live in the Hardcastle Addition, a residential neighborhood in the western section of the Fourth Ward owned by Garrett Sipple Hardcastle (1798–1883), who served as the assessor and collector of taxes for Harris County between 1854 and 1857 and owned Hardcastle & Co. from 1866 to 1869.

Hardcastle was born in Dover, Delaware, and lived in Nashville, Tennessee, before traveling to Houston in 1836, perhaps to join members of his family. Elizabeth Hardcastle Wilson, the mother of Robert Wilson, the original owner of Block 43, was descended from Robert Hardcastle (1711–1760). He had sailed in 1748 from Yorkshire, England, to eastern Maryland, where he established a line of wealthy industrialists and merchants who accumulated real estate in eastern Maryland before spreading out across the United States.[194] Garrett Hardcastle was also descended from Robert Hardcastle, making him Robert Wilson's cousin.

Like Elizabeth Hardcastle Wilson, Garrett Hardcastle was a devout Methodist. He was a charter member of Houston's first Methodist congregation in 1837 and a steward of the church until his death in 1884. In 1838, Augustus Allen gave the Methodists the deed to the "Church Reserve" on Block 58, but they did not build there until 1843. The church for the white congregation faced Texas Avenue and was the first church building in Houston made of brick. The presiding elder preached to the thirty-six white members at 11:00 a.m. on Sundays and to the thirty-two black members in the afternoon. Eventually, the Methodists built a wood-frame church for the black members; it faced Prairie Street and Block 43. After Juneteenth, the freed slaves founded the oldest African American congregation in Houston, today's Trinity United Methodist Church, located at 2600 Holman Street in the Third Ward.[195]

In addition to the land grants he received from the Republic of Texas, Hardcastle acquired property along the north side of the San Felipe Road (today's West Dallas Street) and eventually owned the Hardcastle Addition and the Hopson Addition, where he had his home.[196]

One of the most pressing issues for those who suddenly became freed from the protection and care of their former masters was where would they live. Help came from sympathetic businessmen and influential citizens of Houston. In particular, Garrett S. Hardcastle set aside a tract of land that he owned as a residential development for these newly free persons. The Hardcastle Subdivision soon became known as Freedmanstown....Garrett Hardcastle and other Methodists paid the taxes for freed slaves and helped them keep their properties.[197]

In March 1904, Houston was granted a new city charter by the Texas State Legislature; Houston voters approved the new charter on December 10. It replaced the mayor-alderman form of government with a mayor-commissioner form. At the next election, in 1906, four commissioners were chosen on a citywide basis, not in individual wards, and each commissioner headed a department (water commissioner and fire commissioner). Wards as political subdivisions of the City of Houston were abolished by an ordinance in November 1915.[198]

By the beginning of the twentieth century, black Houstonians could attend schools, colleges, and universities in the United States—if not always in Texas. Many became licensed professionals in order to provide services to their communities during the segregated Jim Crow and pre–civil rights years. Between 1910 and 1925, Block 43's Milam Street was Houston's first African American "downtown" and the center of the city's black professional life. In 1910 and 1911, 409½ Milam Street housed five physicians, a dentist, an attorney, and the offices of the *Texas Freeman*; 419½ Milam Street housed two attorneys, two real estate companies, an architect, a hairdresser, and the offices of the American Mutual Benefit Association and the Western Star printing company. There were three other black insurance companies with offices located near Market Square: the First Texas State Insurance Company, located at 714½ Prairie Street (Block 42), and the Standard American Mutual Fire Insurance Company and the Ancient Order of Pilgrims, both located at 413½ Travis Street (Block 44).

An analysis of the *Houston City Directory of 1923–1924* showed that black businesses were beginning to move farther west in the Fourth Ward, as well as into the Third and Fifth Wards. In 1935, members of the Ancient Order of Pilgrims helped organize the Houston Negro Chamber of Commerce (HNCC), the second black chamber of commerce in the United States. Its headquarters weren't near Market Square but were in a new building that was designed by noted architect Alfred C. Finn and located at Bagby and West Dallas Streets.[199]

Erosion of the community continued after World War II, as downtown Houston began to expand westward. By Sig Byrd's time, the pre–civil rights 1950s,

> *the four hundred block, where the Four Hundred never go,* [was] *called Catfish Reef. The Reef is bi-racial. The light and the dark meet here....* *You can buy practically anything here. Whisky, gin, wine, beer, a one-*

hundred-and-fifty-dollar suit, firearms, a four-bit flop, a diamond bracelet that will look equally good on the arm of a chaste woman or a fun-gal. You can buy fried catfish in Catfish Reef. You can buy reefers on the Reef. Or you can get faded, get your picture made, your shoes shined, your hair cut, your teeth pulled.... The Reef is a quietly cruel street, where rents are high and laughter comes easy, where violence flares quickly and briefly in the Neon twilight, and if a dream ever comes true, it's apt to be a nightmare.[200]

When Sig Byrd wrote, "There is a taxi stand here, and concrete steps mount a curb four feet high," he was describing Block 43. The curbs were made out of bricks left over from the days when shoppers looking for turkey at John Collins' shop hopped off a horse or stepped out of a carriage onto raised sidewalks to avoid the filthy, muddy streets below. "The site on which Houston was founded was not the most hospitable location. The swampy, subtropical setting was a challenge to the early developers," and

Portrait of Members of the Houston Negro Chamber of Commerce, Hicks Collection, MSS0190-0125. Courtesy Houston Metropolitan Research Center, Houston Public Library.

Peter Boesel, "Photo Reference Number 38, Kennedy Bakery, 1982," National Register of Historic Places Inventory— Nomination Form, Main Street/Market Square Historic District, 83004471.

the west side of the City of Houston was particularly undesirable.[201] In 2016, red brick foundations were exposed to a depth of about fifteen feet as Block 43 was excavated in order to make way for a nine-story parking garage at 800 Preston Street, complete with restaurants on the street level. Thanks to the developer's objectives to extend the Downtown Houston Tunnel System to be accessible to Market Square Park and enhance the connectivity between the tunnel level and street level, most of downtown finally is accessible to pedestrians on weekdays, during business hours, regardless of the weather.[202]

THE GHOSTS OF LA CARAFE

The two-story brick building at 813 Congress Street is the oldest intact commercial building in Houston. It was originally called the Kennedy Bakery because its ovens provided "hardtack" for Confederate troops.[203] It was built by John Kennedy (1819–1878), an Irish immigrant and successful businessman. After Kennedy died on Christmas Eve in 1878, his widow, Matilda, inherited the Kennedy Bakery, which by then had become a drugstore. Matilda's death in 1885 was followed by that of her daughter, Mary Frances, the wife of dry goods merchant William L. Foley. W.L. had loaned $2,000 to his Irish nephews, James and Pat Foley, who used it to start what became Foley's department stores and is now a part of the national Macy's chain. Daniel Kennedy, the youngest son of John and Matilda Kennedy, inherited 813 Congress Street and the adjacent alley on the east side of the building. Ownership eventually passed to Daniel's daughter, Ethel Kennedy Bruhl, and then to her grandson Dr. Charles Bruhl.

Over the years, the family rented space in 813 Congress Street to a wide variety of businesses. By 1968, it was home to a small wine bar and bistro called Le Carafe.[204] Two years later, Dr. Bruhl sold the building to businessman William V. Berry (1930–2013), who promptly purchased a huge, antique, red pine bar and changed the bistro to a wine bar called La Carafe. Otherwise, he left the building as he found it, complete with exposed brick walls and wrought-iron-lined windows.

Berry was a man of many parts. He circled the world, first as a captain in the U.S. Air Force and, later, as a helicopter pilot, becoming a serious collector along the way. Today, every wall inside the two-story bar is crammed with photographs, paintings, and memorabilia from the days of Le Carafe and from Berry's travels. Berry also helped create the image of "Old Market Square" that made the neighborhood so popular in the 1970s. At the same time, he turned La Carafe into a unique destination with very old records played on an antique jukebox. To this day, you can select from Marlene Dietrich, Django Reinhardt, Judy Garland, Buddy Holly, Billie Holiday, Otis Redding, Bobby Darin, Duke Ellington, Frank Sinatra, or Bruce Springsteen. In 1986, Berry sold the business and the building to Warren Wenglar and moved to California, where he entered the real estate business and served in the state assembly. He expanded his real estate success from California to Montana, Tennessee, Florida, and then back to Texas, where he died in 2013.[205]

La Carafe's current owner, Carolyn Wenglar, Warren's sister, has operated the bar since Warren's death in 1988. With the help of loyal bartenders, who also are artists and musicians, she has kept La Carafe just as it was, down to the brass, hand-cranked, 1914 National cash register that takes only cash, although she has bowed to the wishes of her customers and installed an ATM machine at the back of the first floor.

Patrons at La Carafe range from bohemians to tourists and the occasional celebrity. Today's crowd may not be familiar with bold-faced names like Liberace, Bill Murray, Dan Aykroyd, Billy Gibbons, or Monica Lewinsky, but they definitely know Queen B and Jay-Z. While the homeless still hang out around the square—many of them so frequently that they have become part of the Market Square "family"—it's best to heed Wenglar's warning: "After the bars close up, it's not real good to be on the street."[206]

In 2002, Marty Racine, then a writer for the *Houston Chronicle*, best described La Carafe:

> *The room is narrow, dark and murky. Old-time ceiling fans stir the natural light filtering through the open front door. The jukebox contains voices from the ages....*[The second floor, accessed] *by a narrow stairway,... appears in afternoon's golden glow like a room out of time: the marble bar, the horse carousel, the stained-glass wall sconces, an old-fashioned cash register, a black vault-like cooler with "ICE" on the front....There is no TV...but there's the moosehead* [near] *the front door....*[On a quiet afternoon at 2:30,] *the moosehead fell to the floor and shattered.... Night doorman Dan Schnoor was sitting beneath it but stood up when he heard footsteps upstairs; no one was supposedly up there. As he moved, the moosehead fell where he'd been sitting...*[Schnoor asked,] *"So why did I get this warning and step back?"* [A bartender explained,] *"It's the ghost of the moose, man."*[207]

Is La Carafe haunted? Only you can judge for yourself. Stories abound about cold spots in the restrooms. Through the years, there have been reports of doors opening on their own, folks seeing "people" out of the corners of their eyes, creaky floorboards, an occasional rolling toy ball, footsteps, glass breaking, and echoes from the second floor of wooden chairs being dragged along the floor or heavy objects moving about.

There have been at least two suicides connected to 813 Congress Street. The first occurred early one morning in 1904. One of the drugstore's employees, fearing a request that he testify in a local court case later that

La Carafe. Photograph courtesy of Sandra Lord.

day, grabbed a folded-up newspaper and went upstairs to the second floor. "A small boy, who stays at the store, was seated in the back room [on the first floor] reading a newspaper, holding it spread out before him. To his dismay, blood began to fall on the paper, coming down in great splotches.... An investigation disclosed the body of the employee lying on the [second] floor." A .38-caliber revolver was found near his body. A bullet "had entered the right side of the head about midway between the eye and the ear." Why did no one hear the gunshot and run upstairs to save the young man's life? The revolver's "report sounded just like the noise produced by" a falling box. When the drugstore's employees emptied a box upstairs, they often threw it on the floor after they removed the last bottle.[208]

The second story took place several years later. It involved a man named E.A. Herring, who, after shaking hands with his best friend near Main and Congress Streets, remarked that it was a "delightful day to end a tired and strenuous life." His friend remembered that Herring turned and walked west along the 900 Block of Congress Street until he reached a barbershop. He stopped and pulled a bottle from his pocket and drank its contents, then threw the bottle into the street. He quickened his pace until he reached Wilbush's Drug Store at 813 Congress Street. He went inside and purchased a bottle of carbolic acid, concealing from the clerk the terrible pain he was suffering. As soon as he stepped outside the front door, Herring swallowed the second bottle's contents, staggered, and fell to the sidewalk. Wilbush's manager rushed outside with a large dose of alcohol, which he hoped might counteract the effects of the acid, but he was too late. Herring died in the arms of a traveling salesman who had been passing by. Newspapers reported later that Herring had received a telegram the night before and a letter that morning, informing him that he had been fired from his job as an insurance salesman.[209]

The most popular ghost story involves Carl Truscott, a longtime manager of La Carafe. Carl died in 1990, but some say he still watches the streets below from the wine bar's second-story window. "A few years back, an employee was getting into his car after closing up and felt the hair on the back of his neck stick straight up. Upon turning around, he spotted a face in an upstairs window. Thinking he might have locked a customer inside the bar, he returned to check it out but could find no one there. The staff at La Carafe believes it was the face of Carl Truscott, who loved the bar so much it is rumored he has never left."[210]

Some paranormal investigators claim that the energies from the old bakery and drugstore linger, creating residual hauntings, past events playing in the present but with no interaction or connection to the present. Due to the strong emotional energy attached to the building, the spirits imprint themselves on the environment where the event took place. They are sort of "trapped in time."

Ghost hunters believe that residual hauntings occur in places built on or near limestone, quartz stone, or water. Note how close La Carafe is to Buffalo Bayou—there is the water source. So, visitors shouldn't be afraid when the floors at La Carafe creak; it's only trapped energy playing back haunted history.

WHO OWNS THIS BUILDING?

As you walk inside 305 Travis Street on Block 33, notice the glass cases to the right, full of finished suits and fabric. On the left are a long cutting table and more glass cases. The hallway leading back to the restrooms is lined with glass cases featuring shirts on the left and ties on the right. The restrooms are joined by fitting rooms. You have definitely entered a tailor shop. But have you?

Michael Shapiro, Owner of Duke of Hollywood Tailors and CharBar. Photograph courtesy of Sandra Lord.

Across from the cutting table is CharBar, a full-service establishment that serves Tuxedo Martinis and frozen margaritas. If it's a Monday, your bartender may be Michael Shapiro, a tailor wearing a yellow tape measure around his neck, standing in front of family photographs that rise up to the ceiling. So, are you in a tailor shop or in a bar? The answer: both. Next question: Are you in one building or in half of one building? If the bar is open, order a cold one and prepare to take notes. The ghosts who haunt 305 and 307 Travis Street are not easy.

The Fox-Kuhlman Building is listed as a contributing building to the Main Street Market Square National Register and City of Houston historic districts. In addition, it was designated a City of Houston Landmark and a Protected Landmark in 2008. Built as one structure between 1862 and 1866, it features two hipped roofs behind a continuous cornice line of decorative brickwork. The two-story brick structure now consists of two separately owned halves: 305 Travis Street, home of the Duke of Hollywood Tailors and CharBar; and 307 Travis Street, home of Warren's Inn. Each half is twenty-five feet wide with three bays. Under divided ownership, the building's front facade has evolved over the years into the appearance of two separate facades, each painted a different color.[211] Why?

In 1837, Lots 9 and 10 in Block 33, the block bounded by Travis, Congress, Preston, and Main Streets, were purchased by Timothy Donnellan and Emilie De Ende, newcomers from New Orleans. Each lot was fifty feet wide and one hundred feet deep. Ten years later, the Donnellans sold off the rear twenty-eight feet of the two lots, thus reducing their depth to seventy-two feet from their frontage on Travis Street. After Timothy's death in 1849, Emilie sold the southern two-thirds of Lot 9 to Thomas Westrope in 1850 and the northern one-third to John Fox in 1851. In 1853, Fox purchased the middle third of Lot 9 so that he and his wife, Eliza, owned the northern two-thirds of Lot 9. Eliza and John Fox had two daughters, Eliza and Francisca (or Frances). The family lived on the second floor of the building and operated a bakery on the ground floor.[212]

After John died in 1854, his widow, Eliza, married widower Charles Stephanes on October 27, 1855. Charles, who had been born in 1806 in Burgundy, France, moved to the Houston area by late 1835, served as a private during the Texas Revolution, and fought at the Battle of San Jacinto on April 21, 1836. In December 1836, he married Catherine Caroline Dunn, the widow of John Conroy, who had been shot by marauding Mexicans. In 1837, Charles opened a grocery store on Market Square. Five years later, Caroline died, leaving behind three children from her second marriage.[213]

Together, Eliza and Charles had a daughter, Mary, around 1857. Their household also included Eliza's three daughters and Charles's three children. Charles purchased the last third of Lot 9 for $600 in 1857. He and Eliza now owned the entire property. In late 1859, after four years of marriage, Eliza petitioned for a divorce from Charles, but on August 20, 1860, before the divorce was granted, a fire destroyed significant portions of the east side of the 300 Block of Travis Street, including Eliza and Charles's homestead and store. When her divorce was finalized on December 22, 1860, Eliza kept the northern two-thirds of Lot 9, her original separate property, as well as the southern one-third of Lot 9 out of her community property with Charles, becoming the sole owner of Lot 9.[214]

Three months later, on March 20, 1861, Eliza married John Kuhlman. He owned the adjacent Lot 10, where he had erected a three-story brick building after the 1860 fire. Like Eliza, Kuhlman was a German immigrant. He was also a widower with several children. As part of their marriage agreement, Eliza transferred the north half of Lot 9 to her third husband. By 1862, Kuhlman had demolished the two-story wood buildings on Lot 9 and begun the construction of a single brick building. Before the new building was completed, however, John and Eliza found themselves "mutually dissatisfied." Since they could not "live agreeably and harmoniously together," on September 23, 1862, they filed a separation agreement in Harris County in which Eliza renounced "all right of habitation with him or in his residence," and Kuhlman surrendered all rights to Lot 9, conveying the partially constructed brick building to Eliza in "its actual condition."[215]

Between the divorce in 1862 and her death in April 1866, Eliza Fox Stephanes Kuhlman completed the construction of the current two-story, two-part brick building on Lot 9. Her estate, which also included numerous other properties, was partitioned among her three daughters. Eliza Thompson and Francisca Schuelby, Eliza's daughters from her marriage with John Fox, were awarded the northern half of Lot 9. Mary Stephanes, Eliza's daughter from her marriage with Charles Stephanes, received the southern half. Each half had a twenty-five-foot frontage on Travis Street, was seventy-two feet deep, and had improvements worth $4,500 in gold.[216] Perhaps it was sometime between 1866 and 1880 that each half of the building was first painted a different color, making it appear as if the one building was actually two separate buildings.

In March 1880, the three sisters sold the entire property to Henry Stude, another German immigrant, for $11,000. He may have continued the tradition of painting the building two different colors. His son and daughter-in-law, Alphonse and Louise Stude, had owned and operated a bakery and coffee "saloon" for many years at 810–812 Preston Street on Block 43, on the south side of Market Square, so he was probably familiar with the building's unique history. After Henry Stude's death in May 1905, ownership of Lot 9 went to his six grandchildren—Henry W., Alphonse, Louis, Stokes, Emilie, and Henrietta—who sold the property to Edward Armstrong for $60,000 in March 1917. Between 1917 and 1936, 305 Travis Street was occupied by grocers, clothing stores, jewelers, pawnbrokers, a harness and saddle maker, real estate offices, and barbers.[217]

Since 1936, 305 Travis Street has been owned by the family of William B. Samuelson, a tailor who moved to Houston in the same year. Samuelson and his son, Lionel, operated Hollywood Tailors out of 305 Travis Street, while his daughter, Udis, married David Shapiro, who had operated Duke's Man's Shop, two doors down at 309 Travis Street, since 1949.[218] When

The Duke of Hollywood Tailors and CharBar both occupy 305 Travis Street. Photograph courtesy of Sandra Lord.

William Samuelson died in 1962, Lionel took over the business. By 1970, he had sold the building to the Shapiros, who merged the two businesses into Duke of Hollywood Tailors at 305 Travis Street in 1971. The Shapiros' grandson, Jeremy, has been trained as a tailor, but he and his sister, Charlien, are not interested in tailoring themselves. "I can always hire a good tailor," Jeremy said a few years back. Instead, he and his sister run CharBar, which opened on June 5, 2002.[219]

On November 8, 2001, Michael Shapiro received a Certificate of Appropriateness from the Houston Archaeological and Historical Commission for the renovations he had made to the exterior of 305 Travis Street. The existing glass block transom windows remained, but the existing aluminum storefront, which had been a later alteration, was replaced with a wood storefront of three bays. The two side bays consist of paired wood doors with elongated vertical glass lights and wood panels below the glass, while the center bay features paired plate glass windows. A decorative wood pilaster was added on the outside edge of the paired doors, and mahogany trim was added around the glass block transom windows.[220]

The south half of the Fox-Kuhlman Building, 307 Travis Street, housed a succession of restaurants and bars until 1988, when it was purchased by Warren Wenglar, who opened Warren's Inn. The bricks are painted turquoise to keep up the over-one-hundred-year tradition of making the two sides of one building appear as if they were two separate buildings.

SPIRITUAL TRAVELERS FIND NEW WORLDS

The spirits of Louisa Margerethe Agnes Schiermann Gerding Hobein Reinermann Sandman Bethje (1813–1867), who married five men in less than twelve years, and Neil Armstrong, the first man to set foot on the moon, may frequent Block 35 on the west side of Market Square Park. Both were intrepid explorers of new worlds.

After her first two husbands died in Germany between 1836 and 1838, twenty-six-year-old Louisa Schiermann Hobein traveled to Bremen,

Peter Boesel, "Photo Reference Number 40, Bethje-Lang Building (ca. 1868), 316 Milam, 1982," National Register of Historic Places Inventory—Nomination Form, Main Street/Market Square Historic District, 83004471.

where she and her daughter, Anna Marie Louisa Gerding (1836–1916), and son, Friedrich Hobein (1838–1862), boarded the *Copernicus* (1835–1846), which was built in 1835 and was engaged in the freight and passenger trade between Bremerhaven and North America.[221] It was named for Nicolaus Copernicus (1473–1543), the Polish mathematician and astronomer who revolutionized concepts of the universe.[222]

Louisa and her 169 companions were also part of a revolution. The *Copernicus* was one of five ships commissioned by the Saxon Auswanderungs-Gesellschaft (Saxon Emigration Society) to take Confessional German Lutherans from Germany to the United States between 1838 and 1839.[223] They arrived in New Orleans on November 18, 1839. From New Orleans, Louisa and her family may have taken the steamboat *Columbia* to Galveston. From Galveston, they may have taken the mail packet *Correo* to Houston.

In Houston, Louisa met Henry Reinermann (1808–1844), who had immigrated to Mexican Texas from Oldenburg, Germany, in 1834, along with his parents, John and Anna Reinermann, and his older brother, John Jr. Although the schooner on which the Reinermann family traveled from New Orleans to Texas was shipwrecked off Galveston Island on December 22, 1834, they found their way to Houston in 1835. They lived in a log cabin surrounded by orchards and cultivated fields on the north side of Buffalo Bayou near today's Memorial Park.[224]

On December 19, 1840, a year after her arrival in Houston, Louisa Schiermann married Henry Reinermann, who legally adopted her two children in 1841 and changed their surnames to Reinermann so that they could inherit his property. Henry died suddenly in 1844, again leaving Louisa a widow with two small children.[225] After Henry's death, his mother, Anna, applied to the Republic of Texas for a headright grant in the name of her deceased husband, John, on the grounds that he was present in Texas before the 1836 revolution.[226] On April 28, 1847, the State of Texas granted John Reinermann's heirs a league (4,338 acres) and labor (177 acres). The John Reinermann League bordered Buffalo Bayou to the south, Reinerman Street to the east, Post Oak Boulevard to the west, and West 15th Street to the north. In addition to their interest in the John Reinermann League, Henry Reinermann's heirs—Louisa and her two children—inherited Henry's land grant of one-third of a league immediately north of his father's land. The boundaries of this property were West 15th Street to the south, West 26th Street to the north, Mangum Road to the west, and Reinerman Street to the east.

Louisa married Joseph Sandman on April 27, 1845. Sandman was one of the original fifty-three members of the first German Society in Texas, which was organized in Houston on November 29, 1840.[227] Louisa gave birth to twins Joseph Sandman Jr. and Josephine in April 1846. Her husband died on October 17, 1846, leaving Louisa a land grant of 640 acres in Austin County, as well as the two-story wood-frame building on Lot 3, Block 35, that he had purchased in 1840. For the fourth time, she was a widow, only now she had two sons and two daughters and a considerable amount of real estate.[228]

In 1847, Louisa married her fifth husband, a farmer named Christian Lodovic Bethje (1822–1876). After little Josephine Sandman died in 1848, Louisa's luck seemed to change, perhaps because her new husband was almost nine years younger than she was or because, together, they eventually owned more than 2,200 acres of land worth $2,250. The couple lived together—happily, we hope—for twenty years on a 20-acre farm with 3 horses, 4 working oxen, 60 milk cows, 140 beeves, and 60 hogs. They also raised watermelons and, in 1850, harvested four hundred bushels of corn.[229]

German-speaking residents represented 45 percent of Houston's citizens, according to the 1850 United States Federal Census. By the end of Reconstruction, Germans no longer accounted for such a large portion of the city's population, but they had become thoroughly established in mercantile enterprises and contributed greatly to local economic growth. "Germans were active in Houston municipal politics; in cultural, religious, and Volksfest celebrations; in fraternal and fire-fighting organizations; and, significantly, in the city's wholesale liquor and saloon trade."[230]

Louisa and Christian had ten children, but only two daughters survived. When Louisa died on October 25, 1867, her estate included more than 4,300 acres of land in four counties.[231] Christian died in 1876. They were buried in the family cemetery on Inker Street until 1910, when their descendants moved them to Glenwood-Washington Cemetery.[232]

Sometime before her death, Louisa replaced the wood-frame building on Block 35, which Joseph Sandman had purchased in 1840, with a two-story brick structure. Later known as the Bethje-Lang Building, 316 Milam Street has had its own colorful history. In 1868, it housed a feed and hardware store. In 1892 and 1893, bartenders Michael Barrett and William H. Higgins rented rooms over John Lacey's "commercial" saloon. The Wilk Hardware Store sold Winchester tools and Charter Oak stoves and ranges there from 1926 until 1967.[233]

New owners of the building in 1967 worked on remodeling it before opening a nightclub named Les Quatre Saisons in 1969. In addition to its French menu, Les Quatre Saisons offered "light and grand opera, with occasional medleys of Broadway show tunes."[234] The *Houston Chronicle*'s society editor, Maxine Mesinger, reported in her Big City Beat column on August 4, 1969, 104 years after Louisa's death, that the club's patrons "got an unexpected thrill" when it was announced that it was "one of Moon astronaut Neil Armstrong's favorite places, and with that, through the use of a phone and a loudspeaker, Armstrong talked to the audience from his home in quarantine at the Manned Spacecraft Center." It was the evening before his thirty-ninth birthday. He had just returned from NASA's Apollo 11 mission to the moon.[235]

Apollo 11 lifted off from Cape Kennedy in Florida on July 16, 1969, carrying Commander Neil Armstrong, Command Module Pilot Michael Collins, and Lunar Module Pilot Edwin "Buzz" Aldrin. On Sunday, July 20, Armstrong and Aldrin entered the Lunar Module [LM] *Eagle.* At 100 hours and 12 minutes into the flight, the *Eagle* undocked and separated from *Columbia*, and at 20:17 UTC, Armstrong announced to Mission Control and the world, "Houston, Tranquility Base here. The *Eagle* has landed," making "Houston" forever the first word spoken from the surface of the moon. Over six hours later, Armstrong exited the LM and walked down the ladder. "At the bottom of the ladder Armstrong said, 'I'm going to step off the LM [lunar module] now.' He turned and set his left boot on the lunar surface at 02:56 UTC July 21, 1969, then said, 'That's one small step for [a] man, one giant leap for mankind.'" Armstrong and Aldrin spent 21 hours and 36 minutes on the moon's surface, then returned in the LM to dock with *Columbia.* After a flight of 195 hours, 18 minutes, and 35 seconds, Apollo 11 splashed down in the Pacific Ocean, thirteen miles from the recovery ship USS *Hornet.*[236] The three astronauts spent eighteen days in quarantine at the Manned Spacecraft Center (today, the Lyndon B. Johnson Space Center) in Houston, then had a "Welcome Home Parade" in downtown Houston on August 16, before departing on September 29 with their wives on a thirty-eight-day "Giant Leap" tour around the world.[237]

Armstrong and his family left NASA and Houston in 1971. On November 18, 2010, at the age of eighty, he said in a speech during the Science & Technology Summit at the Hague, Netherlands, that he would "offer his services as commander on a mission to Mars if he were asked." His family's statement, which was released after he died on August 25, 2012, included the following request: "[T]he next time you walk outside on a clear night and see the moon smiling down at you, think of Neil Armstrong and give him a wink."[238]

Like Armstrong, Louisa would have loved Les Quatre Saisons. Its interior was very ornate, very European. Occasionally, Louisa's spirit may check out her property on Block 35, which is now home to the forty-story Market Square Tower, a luxury apartment with two swimming pools.[239] Spirits

Peter Boesel, "Photo Reference Number 41, Fox-Kuhlman Building (south half) (1862-1866), 307 Travis Street, 1982," National Register of Historic Places Inventory—Nomination Form, Main Street/Market Square Historic District, 83004471.

need energy to manifest, and water transports energy. A chemical engineer once pointed out that although water itself doesn't conduct electricity, the minerals in the water act as conductors. Since spirits only need a small amount of energy to manifest, a swimming pool would provide more than enough mineral-rich water. Would Louisa take a swim in the glass-bottomed pool that juts ten feet out over Preston Street on Market Square Tower's fortieth floor? Any woman who survived five husbands in twelve years would probably wink at the moon and dive right in.[240]

THE GHOST OF WARREN TROUSDALE

Warren Trousdale opened his first downtown bar, the Ali Baba, at 823 Congress Street (the Kennedy Corner) on April 14, 1967. Known for its "fine vintage wines," it closed ten years later. On June 8, 1979, Warren's, a restaurant, opened at 316 Milam Street.[241] Trousdale, no longer a renter depending on annual leases, probably felt safe operating the beautiful restaurant he loved so much. As early as November 26, 1982, however, a development company was attempting to buy the property in order to build a new office building and parking garage. Trousdale's response: "I told them they'd have to build over me because I won't sell. We need some old buildings left, something for future generations to see besides steel and glass—something old and dear."[242]

Warren's Inn, as it was eventually known, was "New Orleans–style ornate, with iron balconies, brick walls, gold-leaf trim and thirty-foot ceilings."[243] It was a building that many Houstonians, including the Urban Animals, a nocturnal group who skated downtown's empty streets, held close to their hearts.[244] That's why the news that Trousdale had sold the property to Guardian Savings came as such an unwelcome surprise. Why had he sold? "Somebody—we don't know who—was putting t-shirts in his toilets (to clog them). They even put cement in his sewer," said his sister, Caroline Wenglar. Deprived of a sewer connection, Warren's Inn closed on December 24, 1987, and moved across Market Square to 307 Travis Street. Warren died in 1988, not long after Guardian Savings demolished the 316 Milam Street building in March—without taking out the proper permits. Only a pile of rubble was left. The oil bust soon caught up to Guardian Savings, and it went bankrupt. "Maybe there was a little bit of karma there," Carolyn Wenglar said at the time.

When Market Square made another comeback in the late 1990s, historic preservation had finally taken hold. A number of historic buildings, including Warren's Inn, were preserved and brought up to code. In 2002, the *Houston Chronicle*'s Marty Racine described a visit to the second Warren's Inn:

> [A] *lime-green building* [with a] *blue neon martini glass* [sign], *boxes piled on the sidewalk, pigeons foraging for scraps. This is a tavern, well off the hip-happening radar screen scanning downtown's revival....Warren's just hunkers down to business—open daily, supported by a loyal base of regulars. It's quiet enough for conversation, even over the jukebox, which is heavy on blues and jazz; no hip-hop, no thudding dance beats. Warren's has no dress code—just come "decently"—and no cover charge. Bartenders tend to stay for years, not months....The brick building, 28 feet shorter than the first Warren's, was built in 1862. It needed roof repairs, and the facade was a drab, unnoticeable green—not that the regulars cared. "The regulars just knew where the door was," Wenglar says. "But I was hearing a lot of people say, 'Well, I can't find you.'" So, she painted it a brighter green. When her brother died at age 62 on May 22, 1988, Wenglar took over, relying on manager Jose Serna, for years the gentlemanly, dapper face of Warren's. Serna, who had been a Warren's customer while living at the Salvation Army for $1 a night, became manager at the first location after alerting Trousdale that employees were diverting the liquor stock. Stricken with cancer, he took his life on Feb. 21, 2000. He was 62. "I miss Jose terrifically," Wenglar says. She began learning the hands-on operation, from cleaning floors to tending bar. No problem: The Bellaire native had always endeavored. She runs a Brazoria County cattle ranch with her husband, Frank; worked in a drugstore, grocery store, credit bureau and bank; taught tap-dancing; and even panned for gold in Alaska.*[245]

Ask a bartender to show you the postcard of Les Quatre Saisons on Milam Street. The old statues and elaborate iron gates are waiting at Wenglar's old family rice farm for a reason to return to Market Square.[246]

BAKER-MEYER BUILDING GHOSTS

The Baker-Meyer Building is a Protected Landmark dating back to the 1870s.[247] Next to the Kennedy Bakery (La Carafe) and the Fox-Kuhlman

Building (Hollywood Tailors/CharBar/Warren's Inn), it is the third-oldest commercial building in Houston.[248] The building's original owner, George Frederick Baker (1812–1890), emigrated with his family from Baden-Baden, Germany, to Harrisburg, Pennsylvania, where he became a butcher. In 1834, he traveled south to New Orleans, and four years later, at the age of twenty-six, he made Houston his home. His real estate acumen proved that the one thing George Baker did better than butchering was acquire land. There was no secret to his success. "Through every step from poverty to wealth, he rigidly practiced the precepts of 'Poor Richard.'" He worked hard, lived within his income, saved his money, and made judicious investments. "He looked closely after details, and he avoided debt as one would the plague."[249]

Perhaps George Baker arrived in Houston in 1838 on a steamboat captained by Mr. Sterett, the river pilot who had invited John James Audubon and his party on board to dry off in May 1837. A year after Baker's arrival, fifteen-year-old John Washington Lockhart took Sterett's steamboat from Galveston to Houston. In his memoir, *Sixty Years on the Brazos*, Lockhart described how Sterett headed north into Galveston Bay early in the morning. After crossing two sandbars without incident, they passed Lynchburg and the site of the Battle of San Jacinto, where "every eye strained," trying to identify where the Texans had made their opening charge and where so many Mexican soldiers drowned in the marsh next to Galveston Bay.[250]

> [N]*ight overtook us as we entered the narrows of Buffalo bayou, then a miserable stream for navigation....It seemed that our boat entered with a very tight squeeze....Captain Sterett had two huge bonfires made, one for each side of the bow of the boat of pine knots. These fires were made in iron baskets, supported on iron rods attached to the bow, so that the boat in moving along carried its own light. These lights in straight parts of the bayou lit up for some distance, but when the boat would have to make short curves in following the winding stream the bow would frequently appear to rest on one bank of the bayou and the stern on the other, and then the lights would make it appear as if we were about to take to the woods. All trace of water was gone until the deck hands, with their long poles would, by pushing against the bank, turn the prow of the boat into the stream again. At these times the boat, gliding smoothly and almost without noise along the banks, the torches casting grewsome [sic] shadows of the big trees here and there, the thumping of the machinery, the ringing of the bells signaling the engineer to "go ahead" or "reverse," mixed with the wild refrain of the boat hands singing their chorus songs; the darkness and stillness of the night outside, except when broken*

by the occasional howl of some wild animal, made one feel as if he were wandering in dreamland....We Landed At Houston at about 8 o'clock in the morning...Captain Sterett made his boat fast to a large cypress tree standing near the water, and also near the foot of Main street....Everything around the landing place was in a state of nature except a portion of the steep bluff had been scraped off sufficiently for a roadway for drays and carts to get to the sand bar, which had been converted into a wharf.

George Baker was described by one historian as "very much a man unto himself." He and his second wife, Rebecca Stringer (1819–1915), and their ten children lived west of the city, along the San Felipe Road (now West Dallas Street) on a large ranch that had been started with Sam Houston's "rancho" and eventually included farmland, grazing land for cattle, and pens that fed his local slaughterhouse operation. When he died, George Baker was one of the wealthiest property owners in Harris County. Like Charlotte Allen and many other Houston pioneers, he and his family are buried at Glenwood Cemetery.[251]

When Baker was forty-six years old, he and his wife had their seventh child, a daughter named Rebecca after her mother. By 1884, it was time for Rebecca Baker (1858–1915) to find a husband. Like Charlotte Marie Baldwin Allen, Rebecca was in danger of being a spinster at age twenty-six

Baker-Meyer Building, 315 Travis Street. Photograph courtesy of Sandra Lord.

when she married Joseph Francis Meyer (1851–1935). Luckily, her match turned out much better than Charlotte's. Joseph Francis Meyer also was born in Baden-Baden, Germany, and immigrated to the United States as a child. His family settled in St. Louis, Missouri, and Memphis, Tennessee, before moving to Houston in 1867. When his father died the next year, Joseph took over the hardware business and became the head of his family's household at the tender age of sixteen.

In the early 1870s, Joseph's stepmother, Mary Meyer, lived in a Gulf Coast cottage at 313 West Dallas Street, site of today's C. Baldwin Hotel. Her other children, William and Amelia, lived with them. Joseph enlarged the house by using recycled crates from his business to add a second story. He moved out after his marriage in 1884, but the structure remained in the Meyer family until 1940. It was donated to the city in 1962 and moved to Sam Houston Park, where it was restored by Houston architect Harvin C. Moore.[252]

Starting small and growing carefully, Joseph Meyer sold heavy hardware, wagonmakers' supplies, farm implements, railroad contractors' supplies, iron, and steel. By the time he married Rebecca, Joseph Meyer's was one of the largest hardware companies in Harris County. In 1885, Meyer began acquiring land in the southwest part of Houston, and by 1893, he owned more than six thousand acres.[253]

George Baker considered his Greek Revival building on Block 33 an investment property. He already had a butcher shop in Stall No. 54 at the City Market on Block 34. His two-story, brick Baker Block had replaced Sam Houston's office on Lots 9 and 10 of Block 43 with a grocery and feed store, dry goods store, saloon, and barbershop on the ground floor and dwellings above, where his boarders could take in the view from an iron balcony. Perhaps Baker's new building included a corbelled brick cornice and iron balcony on the second floor to attract more upscale tenants like Renzo Greunewald. The Greunewald family had been in the music business in New Orleans since 1852 and expanded to Houston in 1870. Their shop occupied both 313 and 315 Travis Street. Pianos, organs, and imported sheet music in French, German, and Italian were displayed through the large glass windows on the first floor. Music teachers held classes on the second floor.[254]

Between 1877 and 1980, shops in the Baker-Meyer Building have ranged from a bowling alley in 1907 to hardware stores, tin shops, feed stores, drugstores, toy stores, clothing stores, shoe shops, hat shops, and, beginning in the mid-1920s, tailor shops. A 1968 or 1969 photograph recently surfaced on Instagram showing Griff's Green Derby restaurant and Irish pub operating in 313 and 315 Travis Street, next to Polmer's Tailoring Shop on the first and second floors of 317 Travis Street. Other restaurants, saloons, bars, and nightclubs have included Café Sauter and Lang's Oyster Parlor, as well as the Super Market and Le Bon Rat in the swinging 1960s and 1970s. By 1975, the entrance to 315 Travis Street was boarded up, and a "For Rent" sign was put in front of the door. The "Square" was, "for all practical purposes, dead."[255]

Dan Tidwell opened the original Treebeards, a thirty-seat "southern comfort" café, in March 1978, on Block 44. Within a year, he was joined by accountant Jamie Mize. They quickly outgrew the small space and moved to the first floor of the Baker-Meyer Building in 1980. For thirty years, Jamie and Dan gradually expanded Treebeards before selling it in 2010 to new owners who had grown up with the restaurant. When Treebeards in Market Square closed on June 26, 2020, it may have held the record as the Baker-Meyer Building's longest first-floor tenant.[256] Renters on the second floor were more reliable. Polmer's Tailoring Shop was located there for about fifty years.

Houston's population exploded after World War II, from 646,869 people in 1940 to 947,500 in 1950.[257] Ex-serviceman Gerald Danowitz (1919–1994) was one of the newcomers. Born in Harrisburg, Pennsylvania, he became a warrant officer in the U.S. Army during World War II. After separating from the service in 1945, he headed to New Orleans to meet up with his old friend Meyer Gus Rex Braun (1921–1975), who had been born in Houston but was living in New Orleans after serving with the U.S. Marine Corps.

Gerald went on a blind date with Dorothy Reiner (1922–2006) and married her on November 18, 1945. Even before Dorothy and Gerald decided to get married, her father, Nathan Reiner, had made plans to leave the family's successful jewelry company in New Orleans for Houston and lease space at 305 Travis Street. Rex married his sweetheart, Ruth Sacks (1927–2015), in 1945 in New Orleans, where he had become a salesman for Polmer's Tailoring Company. Gerald arrived in Houston first and leased space for a Houston branch of Polmer's Tailoring Company at 313 Travis Street. Rex and Ruth joined him in 1947.

Tailors were among the first merchants to set up shop after Houston's founding. Mary Austin Holley, Stephen F. Austin's distant cousin, noted that Houston men "dressed remarkably well, clothes being bought from New York made in the newest fashion."[258] They could purchase dry goods— cottons, wool, silks, and linens—as well as a variety of manufactured items of dress from several local merchants who imported their wares from New Orleans, New York, London, France, and beyond.

Eventually, Rex branched out on his own. A marker in the sidewalk in front of the doorway at 313 Travis Street commemorates "Rex the Tailor," where Ruth and Rex "worked side by side" until his death in 1975. When Rex took off for Austin to serve as a Texas state representative from the Twenty-Third District during the sixtieth, sixty-first, and sixty-second legislatures, Ruth continued to run the business.[259] In 1971, during the sixty-second session, Rex gained fame as a member of the "Dirty Thirty," thirty-five members of the Texas House of Representatives who, although they were a clear minority in the 150-member house, "put aside party loyalty to force out Speaker Gus Mutscher, who ruled the chamber like a dictator.... Even more unlikely, perhaps, is that they were successful....The next year, Mutscher resigned, marking at least one instance in which the little guys actually won."[260] Since tailors, like hairdressers and barbers, keep their clients' secrets, and since city officials, attorneys, and the media made up a significant percentage of the two tailors' clientele, it is probable that they knew a lot more about what was happening and why than they let on.

As each tailor retired, Treebeards acquired his space, eventually occupying all of the second floor. Not long afterward, the hauntings began. Anh Tran, one of the bean cooks, said that when he opened up the restaurant in the morning, he would often hear someone walking around upstairs, even though the place was unoccupied. After checking to see who might have come in before him, he never found anyone there. Tran's story was corroborated by other Treebeards employees who said they "heard the sounds of phantom footsteps in unoccupied areas of the restaurant, as well as soft voices speaking inaudibly, just out of earshot." Some of them even reported seeing the ghost climbing the stairs at 317 Travis Street. The man they all described, Jamie and Dan realized, sounded just like Mr. Danowitz.[261]

A Houston-based paranormal team, 39 Ghost Hunters, once did an investigation at Treebeards. After they placed a K2 EMF meter on a table on the second floor, its blinking lights began to respond to their questions. When Joey Longa, then a reporter with Houston's Channel 39, asked, "Do you want us to leave?" the meter blinked as if to say "yes." One team member reported that he felt as though someone was following him as he walked down the stairs to the first floor.[262] Some ghosts appear to have strong emotional ties to a site, especially if it was a thriving business and they enjoyed interacting with their customers on a daily basis. The Baker-Meyer Building's ghosts—Rex, Ruth, and Gerald—are just coming around to see that the cleaning and pressing are in order. Like the other ghosts in and around Market Square Park, they are nothing to be afraid of.

Market Square Park, March 2019. Courtesy of Aryelle Amador.

When the south wall of the building started to crumble in 2011, the popular 1997 market scene mural by local painter Suzanne E. Sellers disappeared behind a new wall of concrete blocks that was added for stability. At about the same time, Houston First, the organization that promotes Houston, was looking for a large, prominent wall on which to place a new mural featuring the city's diverse attractions. The building's owners made a handshake agreement to lease the wall to Houston First, which then commissioned *Houston Is Inspired* by local artist GONZO 247. Since its completion in May 2013, the corner of Preston and Travis Streets has become a popular photo-op stop.

The Baker-Meyer Building is unique; not only does it date back to the 1870s, it also has been preserved by descendants of its original owner, George Frederick Baker, who have shown up, day after day, year after year, to watch over Houston. Thanks to them and a multitude of others who have worked to save Houston's history, the area around Houston's Market Square Park is no longer a ghost town.

A Short Guide to the Paranormal

Afterlife. Life after our physical bodies die.

Anomaly. Deviation from the normal, something that is out of place and unexplained.

Apparition. When a spirit takes on a physical form that can be seen, or an anomalous, quasi-perceptual experience. Apparitions retain some elements of the human after death and, at least under certain circumstances, can make themselves perceptible to living human beings. They are the disembodied souls of deceased creatures. It is important to commend the spirit associated with the site and politely ask it to reveal itself. Sometimes, you can't see an apparition with your naked eye, but you can see it on a digital camera. *See also: Ghost.*

Audible Symptoms. One or more voices heard when no one is present. Audible symptoms may be intelligible or unintelligible.

Aura. The emanation of energy that surrounds all living things.

Automatic Writing. Phenomenon by which people write without conscious thought.

Battery Drain. A spirit can drain energy from fully charged batteries so that it can become manifest.

Benign Spirit. A spirit that is not harmful; a spirit guide or an angel.

Channeling. The process that mediums use to communicate with the deceased.

Clairvoyance. The psychic ability to see events which have yet to occur. *See also: ESP.*

Cold Spot. An area where the temperature is lower than it is in the surrounding environment. Cold spots are believed to be created when a ghost is present. An entity that drains thermal energy from an area in order to accomplish some form of manifestation. (Think Patrick Swayze's character in the movie *Ghost.*) *See also: Kinetic Symptoms.*

Demon. An inferior deity often spoken of in religious texts as pure evil.

Disembodied. A spirit that is heard but has no physical body. *See also: EVP.*

Dowsing. Interpreting the motions of rods, sticks, pendulums, and other instruments to obtain information.

Market Square Park, March 2019. Courtesy of Aryelle Amador.

Ectoplasm. A substance that emanates from a medium during a trance. It often appears as a mist-like or vaporous substance. It can be seen moving. Sometimes, faces and other forms can be seen in it. A wispy or foggy, vaporous image captured by video or still cameras.

Electromagnetic Field (EMF). An electric and magnetic energy that radiates from radio and light waves to gamma and cosmic rays. Paranormal activity is considered to be present when an EMF detector or sensor reads between two and ten milligauss.

Electronic Voice Phenomenon (EVP). The use of audio equipment to capture voices and sounds of the dead when there are no physical presences in the area where the recordings are taken. We suggest using a fresh tape of no more than ninety minutes in length. Never use your recorder's on-board microphone; it can catch the sound of the recorder's internal mechanisms on the tape. Place your external microphone at least three feet from the recorder. *See also: Disembodied.*

EMF Detector. A device that measures and detects changes in the electromagnetic field; they are used to measure a ghost's magnetic energy.

Exorcism. The expulsion of ghosts, demons, spirits, or other entities that are believed to disturb or possess a person or a place that people frequent.

Extrasensory Perception (ESP). The ability to receive information about past, present, or future events that cannot be obtained through the normal senses. *See also: Clairvoyance.*

Gauss Meter. A device that is used to measure the electromagnetic field, also referred to as an EMF detector.

Ghost. A ghost is believed to be the soul, life force, or apparition of a person who died tragically, especially by murder or suicide, and can't accept their death—someone who has unfinished earthly business or is guilt-plagued. Ghosts can be interactive (intelligent) or residual. They can be earthbound for a short while, for centuries, or for all of eternity. *See also: Apparition, Residual.*

Ghost Hunt. A conscious effort to search for a known ghost; visiting places you suspect are haunted.

Ghost Investigation. Going into an area in order to look for ghosts or hauntings under controlled conditions. It is important to create reports to document the event, listing all the equipment readings along with time, weather, and temperature as the project unfolds. These reports create valuable information for later research.

Haunted, Haunting. A person, place, or object a spirit is attached to. The spirit can be human or inhuman. Paranormal phenomena, such as apparitions, unexplained sounds, smells, or other sensations, that are associated with a specific location over a long period of time. Paranormal activity around a person or location that is caused by an intelligent or conscious spirit with the capacity to interact with living beings. Classic evidence includes having your name called when no one is there or having items appear and disappear in strange locations.

Interactive (Intelligent) Spirit. An independent and conscious spirit with the capacity to interact with living beings. The theory is that "spirit forms" vibrate at a much higher rate than we do and are therefore virtually invisible to the naked eye. When you feel the presence of an intelligent spirit, you should wear something made of silver, pray for protection from your favorite "god or goddess" or angel or spirit guide, or simply ask the specter to depart. Don't antagonize it by shouting or cursing.

IR (Infrared). Typically, light in the wavelength range of 750 nm to 2,000 nm. An infrared thermometer uses infrared technology to measure the temperature of a surface or the ambient temperature of an area. A thermal scanner provides an infrared image of temperatures in the area. Both can be used to find cold spots.

K2 Meter. Picks up energy fields that spirits disturb when they are present.

Kinetic Symptoms. Activities involving an obvious change to the physical world that can run the gamut of human possibility. A short list would include items being moved a measurable distance, thrown across the room, slid across a surface, or off the surface and items being hidden from residents or their guests. Mechanical equipment or fixtures can be activated without anyone being near them, such as toilets flushing, sinks and showers turning on and off, light switches flipping themselves on, drawers and doors opening and closing, or locks engaging and disengaging. *See also: Cold Spot.*

Market Square Park, March 2019. Courtesy of Aryelle Amador.

Manifestation. Appearing as or taking on the form of an entity.

Medium. A person who acts as a bridge between the living and the dead.

Near-Death Experience (NDE). Experiences people have after they have been pronounced clinically dead or have been very close to death.

Night Vision™. A trademarked technology that enables vision at night by amplifying low light in order to create visible images or detect infrared wavelengths.

Orb. A translucent, spherical mass of energy resembling a ball or globe of light. Orb colors can range from white and red to neon. Seeing an orb is considered the first stage of spirit manifestation.

Paranormal. Phenomena that seem to defy the known laws of science.

Poltergeist. A German word that means "noisy or mischievous ghost." It can be a destructive spirit that has the ability to move objects by solidifying the ambient air, resulting in the movement or teleportation of objects.

Portal. A theoretical doorway of energy through which spirits may be able to enter or exit a location.

Psychic. A person with the ability to see, hear, and feel using senses other than natural senses.

Residual Energy. Emotionally charged events that leave an imprint or energy residue on nearby physical objects. The energy repeats constantly, as if on a loop, and while the energy levels may increase or decrease, the content remains the same with each manifestation.

Residual Haunting. Believed to be a psychic imprint of a scene that keeps repeating itself. The spirit does not interact with humans. Instead, something resembling a recording is made; then, when conditions are right, the walls or earth will "play back" what they have "recorded." There is nothing intelligent behind the haunting; it's left over from a repeated or highly emotional activity.

Shapeshifting. The paranormal ability to assume the form of another person, animal, or entity.

Specter. A ghost or apparition.

Spike. A sudden and unexplainable jump on an EMF meter, causing it to quickly rise and fall or "peg" the meter.

Spirit. A spirit is believed to exist in an invisible realm that can be seen only under certain circumstances or by people with special abilities.

Thermal Scanner. Scanning probe microscopy that maps the local temperature and thermal conductivity of an interface. The probe in a scanning thermal microscope is sensitive to local temperatures, providing a nanoscale thermometer.

Visual Symptoms. Apparitions, hazes or mists, orbs, shadows, and shapes that are often seen out of the corner of the eye, but they are sometimes seen in the center of your vision.

Vortex. A swirling funnel shape when in motion. It can also appear as long and narrow and having a tread-like design. Some people theorize that this is a vehicle to transport spirits in the shape of orbs from their realm to ours. A linear anomaly made up of several orbs in a photograph; they can appear to hover or be in motion.

ACKNOWLEDGEMENTS

There is no way Sandra and Debe could have written this book without substantial help from others. They would like to thank, in particular: Ben Gibson, their editor, and all of the staff at The History Press who patiently read countless emails, provided excellent advice, and made this book possible.

The knowledgeable staff members at the Houston Metropolitan Research Center of the Houston Public Library, the Harris County Archives, the University of Houston's Special Collections, Rice University's Woodson Research Center, the Museum of Fine Arts–Houston, the San Jacinto Museum of History's Albert and Ethel Herzstein Library, the Stephen F. Austin State University's East Texas Research Center, and the University of Texas at Austin's Dolph Briscoe Center for American Studies.

Sculptor Lori Betz, who donated the images of her statues of the Allen brothers at the Smith Street entrance to City Hall, and photographers Aryelle Amador, Peter Wier, and Linda Pham.

Last but not least, Sandra would like to thank Alexandra, Alfred, Emily, and Aryelle, the wind beneath her wings. Debe would like to thank Kenton, her significant other from Texas who kept her curious enough about the legends, lore, and haunts of the Houston area to contact Sandra in 2005.

They take full responsibility for any errors.

NOTES

Chapter 1

1. Southwick, "Robert Wilson," 8.
2. Dittman, *Allen's Landing*, 696–97. Dr. Dittman is a descendant of the fifth Allen brother, George Allen (1815–1854).
3. Southwick, "Robert Wilson," 20.
4. Roark, "Robert Wilson," iii.
5. *History of Texas*, 437.
6. Roark, "Robert Wilson," 2. Margaret's last name was spelled variously as Pendergrass, Pendergrast, Prendergrass, Prendergrast, and Prendergast. She was also known as Bernice.
7. Ibid., 3, 20.
8. Schermerhorn and Schermerhorn, *Business of Slavery*, 17.
9. Wikipedia, "Bateau."
10. Wikipedia, "Steamboats"; Brasseaux and Fontenot, *Steamboats*, 8.
11. Roark, "Robert Wilson," 4.
12. Ibid., 5; Southwick, "Robert Wilson," 8.
13. Wikipedia, "Mill (grinding)." Sawmills process timber into lumber, while gristmills process grains into flour. The first mills were powered by humans and animals. Watermills, which date back to at least 323 BCE in ancient Greece, revolutionized civilization by harnessing natural forces such as wind and water. Most mills today, such as steel mills, are powered by electricity. In Harrisburg, "early grist and sawmills were set in the streambed in order to create water power using waterfalls. Some created water sluices to fill lakes for water power." As soon as steam was available, mills like the sawmill and gristmill built by Robert Wilson "converted their operations to the higher power machinery"; Janet K. Wagner, "Harrisburg."

14. Carroll, *History of Houston*, 342; Southwick, "Robert Wilson," 9.

15. Southwick, "Robert Wilson," 9.

16. Sarah Reed and Sarah Deel are the names given to Robert Wilson's second wife on the documents the authors consulted. They may not be accurate. Roark, "Robert Wilson," 8–10. Wilson Road ran east along the northern shore of Clear Lake, through orchards and cattle-grazing country in Harris and Galveston Counties. In 1962, it was renamed NASA Road One, as the Wilson land grants became part of the United States' Manned Spacecraft Center; Southwick, "Robert Wilson," 9–10; Cherry, "50th Anniversary."

17. Roark, "Robert Wilson," 20.

18. Barker and Pohl, "Revolution."

19. Nance, "Republic."

20. The brass plaque affixed to a granite boulder bears the names and offices of the six men who were members of Jane Harris's household from March 23 to April 13, 1836, when it served as the capitol of the Republic of Texas. The boulder and a flagpole flying the Texas flag were dedicated at the site of Jane Harris's home by the Daughters of the Republic of Texas on May 4, 1929. The boulder can still be found in the 600 Block of Frio Street near Brady's Island on Houston's East End.

21. Adapted from Dittman, *Allen's Landing*, 697–98.

22. Texas Almanac, "National Capitals of Texas"; McGinty, "Steamboat," 14–17.

23. Dittman, *Allen's Landing*, 697–98. To take a sounding means to measure the depth of water with a sounding line or lead line—a length of thin rope with a plummet, generally of lead, at its end. It is common practice to tie marks at intervals along the lines to make it easier to "read" them; www.wikipedia.org.

24. Wikipedia, "Long Expedition." A filibuster or "freebooter" is any irregular soldier who conducts a private, unauthorized military expedition into a foreign country or territory to foment or support a revolution. The terms are rooted in the Dutch word *vrijbuiter.* The Long Expeditions were unsuccessful attempts led by filibuster James Long, an American physician, between 1819 and 1821 to take control of Spanish Texas. In the summer of 1819, after briefly establishing a Republic of Texas (the first use of that sovereign name), Long's filibusters were driven out of Mexico by Spanish troops. When he returned to Texas in 1820 with another army in an attempt to reestablish the Republic, Long was captured and imprisoned in 1821; he was killed by a guard in Mexico City on April 8, 1822.

25. Texas State Historical Association, "Austin, John Punderson." There is no genealogical evidence that Stephen F. Austin's and John Austin's families were related in the United States; Worrall, *Pleasant Bend*, 28.

26. A league is 4,338 acres. A labor is 177 acres. Roark, "Robert Wilson," 43; Southwick, "Robert Wilson," 14; Writers' Program, Works Progress Administration in the State of Texas, *Houston*, 37.

27. Elizabeth Ellet Austin Parrott became a widow again in 1839; she was married in 1845 for the third and last time to William Pierpont (1797–1866). William was born in Hartford, Connecticut. He had come to Austin's Colony with his first wife, Sophronia Frisbie, in 1835 or 1836. Sophronia died on May 28, 1840, at their

Cottage Hill Plantation near Lynchburg. William's mother, Rhoda Collins (1764–1845), and her sister, Elizabeth (1755–1815), married two Pierpont brothers. Rhoda married Evelyn Pierpont (1755–1809), who was a direct descendant of the Duke of Kingston. The Duke was an ancestor of Catherine, the Duchess of Cambridge and wife of William, Prince of Wales. Elizabeth Collins married Evelyn's brother James (1761–1840), whose granddaughter, Juliet Pierpont (1816–1884), married Junius Spencer Morgan (1813–1890). Their oldest son was John Pierpont Morgan (1837–1913)—J.P. Morgan.

28. Dittman, *Allen's Landing*, 697–98; Southwick, "Robert Wilson," 14; MacCorquodale, "Purchase Price," 12; Davie, *Early History*, 8; Deed Records of Harris County, A, 157–58, 163.

29. G. and T.H. Borden, *Telegraph and Texas Register* 1, no. 49, eds. 1 and 3 (Tuesday, December 27, 1836), www.texashistory.unt.edu; crediting the Dolph Briscoe Center for American History.

30. Looscan, "Beginnings of Houston," 52; Davie, *Early History*, 11; Albert and Ethel Herzstein Library, San Jacinto Museum of History, "Moses Lapham"; Frantz, "Moses Lapham," 468.

31. Texas State Historical Association, "Day by Day."

32. Winkler, "Seat of Government," 160–68.

33. Legislative Reference Library of Texas, *Journals*, 213.

34. Hinton, *Houston Streets*, 131, 148. The first map of Houston shows "Streets" running from north to south and "Avenues" running from west to east. Today, the U.S. Postal Service designates all streets in downtown Houston as "Streets."

35. Williams and Barker, "Houston to Robert A. Irion, January 23, 1837," 48; Roark, "Robert Wilson," 43–44; Southwick, "Robert Wilson," 14.

36. Legislative Reference Library, *Journals*. Today, Lot 7 on Block 33 is home to the Baker-Meyer Building (1870s) at 313–317 Travis Street, and Lot 8 is split between the Alltmont Building (1879) at 311 Travis Street and the Larendon Building (1890–1896) at 309 Travis Street.

37. Washington-on-the-Brazos State Historical Foundation, "Texas Capitals."

38. Carroll, *History of Houston*, 30.

39. Farrar, *Story of Buffalo Bayou*, 8–9. Today, the first lot sold in Houston, Lot 3, Block 19, is home to Henke & Pillot (www.henkehouston.com), a chic gastropub that serves a range of classic and modern cocktails along with creative bar fare; Carroll, *History of Houston*, 28–29, 65; Lubbock, *Six Decades*, 45–47.

40. Hafertepe, *French Legation*, 1; Lubbock, *Six Decades*, 48; Cruger and Moore, *Telegraph and Texas Register* 3, no. 14, ed. 1 (Saturday, March 17, 1838) www.texashistory.unt.edu; University of North Texas Libraries, the Portal to Texas History, www.texashistory.unt.edu; crediting the Dolph Briscoe Center for American History.

41. Glass, "Book of Sales," 182; Johnston, *Houston*, 11–12.

42. Hans Peter Mareus Neilsen Gammel, "An Act to Incorporate the Town of Nacogdoches and other Texas Towns herein named," *The Laws of Texas, 1822–1897* Volume 1, (Austin, TX: University of North Texas Libraries, 1898), www.texashistory.unt.edu, 238–39.

43. The value of $80,000 in 1837 was $2,054,525 in 2019 currency, according to the Official Data Foundation's Consumer Price Index Calculator; Works Progress Administration, *Houston*, 285–86; Holman, "Houston City Lots," 2–3; Glass, "Book of Sales," note 6, 168.
44. Glass, "Book of Sales," note 5, 167, 168.
45. Williams and Barker, *Writings of Sam Houston*, 182–83.
46. John Kirby Allen is buried with other family members in Founders Memorial Cemetery at 1217 West Dallas Street; Works Progress Administration, *Houston*, 140; Glass, "Book of Sales," note 10, 168–69; Williams and Barker, *Writings of Sam Houston*, 184.
47. Williams, "Allen."
48. Ibid.
49. Ibid.
50. Ibid.
51. Glass, "Book of Sales," note 53, 189; Jones, "Allen"; Joe Holley, "Allen Brothers."
52. Works Progress Administration, *Houston*, 38; Wikipedia, "Saw Pit." "A sawpit is a large hole over which lumber is positioned to be sawed with a long, two-handled saw by two people, one standing above the timber and the other below. A sawpit could produce sawn planks from tree trunks, which could then be cut down into boards, pales, posts, etc."; Henson, "Boyce," 30; Boyce, "Memoir," 38.
53. "Recess" was a medieval English term for a communal, secluded storage building for farm products and arms, according to *A New English Dictionary on Historical Principles*, 8; Works Progress Administration, *Houston*, 246–48.
54. Cruger and Moore, *Telegraph and Texas Register* 2, no. 34, ed. 1 (Saturday, September 2, 1837) www.texashistory.unt.edu, 3; University of North Texas Libraries, the Portal to Texas History, www.texashistory.unt.edu; crediting the Dolph Briscoe Center for American History.
55. Ibid.; Carroll, *History of Houston*, 77–78.
56. Scardino, "Legacy," 154–64.
57. Ibid.; Carroll, *History of Houston*, 77–78; Works Progress Administration, *Houston*, 246–48.
58. Carroll, *History of Houston*, 77–78; Scardino, "Legacy," 154–64.
59. "Historical," in *Mooney and Morrison's Directory of the City of Houston for 1877–1878* (Houston, TX: W.M. Hamilton, 1877), 15; Howe-Houghton, Scardino, Blackburn, and Howe, *Forgotten Heritage*, 274.
60. *City Directory for 1866.*
61. Moneyhon, *Republicanism*, 12.
62. Works Progress Administration, *Houston*, 81.
63. Cushing, "City."
64. Foner, "Civil War and Reconstruction."
65. Ibid.
66. Davis, *Houston*, 19.

67. Wikipedia, "Alexander McGowan." McGowan was one of the few people who served three or more terms as Houston's mayor—1858, 1867, and 1868; Leonard, *City Directory*, 27; Merseburger, "Political History," 8–13, 35.

68. Wikipedia, "John Robert Morris"; Leonard, *City Directory*, 27; Merseburger, "Political History," 13.

69. Works Progress Administration, *Houston*, 246–48; Carroll, *History of Houston*, 77–78.

70. Moneyhon, *Republicanism*, 122; Leonard, *City Directory*, 28; Johnston, *Houston*, 77; Merseburger, "Political History," 99–105.

71. Robinson, "Temples," 454–55. The architect may have been Carl de Grote. In 1871, the State of Texas hired de Grote as the second architect for the first building on its new agricultural and mechanical college campus. According to Ernest Langford in *Getting the College Underway* (College Station, 1970), "[t]he first architectural work was evidently done by C.G. Forshey early in 1871. Later that year, Carl de Grote's plans were accepted but he, in turn, was replaced by [Jacob] Larmour [of Austin]....[After an] inspection in late 1871 revealed...an 'irregular, not level, cracked and unsafe foundation,' de Grote was dismissed because of 'defective plans'"; McCoy and Woodcock, *Architecture*, 2.

72. Scardino, "Legacy," 154–64; "Houston Local," *Galveston Daily News*, 3.

73. Merseburger, "Political History," 127–28; Works Progress Administration, *Houston*, 246–48.

74. Platt, *City Building*, 36; Works Progress Administration, *Houston*, 86.

75. Carroll, *History of Houston*, 78, 108. Carroll wrote that the first City Hall "was not only the first really substantial building of the kind erected here," it was the first one in Houston, "in the construction of which, what has come to be known as 'high finance' methods were employed"; Scardino, "Legacy," 154–64; Merseburger, "Political History," 128.

76. Green, *Fire Fighters*, 123.

77. *Houston City Directory, 1917*, 117, 284.

78. Platt, *City Building*, 40. The value of $100,000 (in 1871) was $2,099,532 in 2019 currency, according to the Official Data Foundation, Consumer Price Index Calculator.

79. Carroll, *History of Houston*, 77–78.

80. Merseburger, "Political History," 130.

81. Architectural Styles of America and Europe, "Second Empire." "Second Empire" refers to the reign of Napoleon III (1852–1870), who "undertook a major building campaign to transform Paris into a city of grand boulevards and monumental buildings."...His enlargement of the Louvre (1852–1857) "reintroduced the Mansard roof, developed during the 1600s Renaissance by Francois Mansart. By the 1860s, the style diffused from France to Britain, and into the United States by way of Boston—at that time America's cultural capital"; Scardino, "Legacy," 154–64; Merseburger, "Political History," 151.

82. Fox, "Houston Buildings," 3. The architect could have been either Charles Emerson Hoar or Carl de Grote; Scardino, "Legacy," 154–64; Carroll, *History of Houston*, 78; Works Progress Administration, *Houston*, 246–48; Chew, "City Council," 7; Merseburger, "Political History," 214, 241; Chew, J.C. *Houston Telegraph* 38, no. 45, ed. 1 (Thursday, March 13, 1873) www.texashistory.unt. edu; University of North Texas Libraries, the Portal to Texas History, www. texashistory.unt.edu; crediting the Dolph Briscoe Center for American History.

83. Carroll, *History of Houston*, 78, 108.

84. Merseburger, "Political History," 157. Works Progress Administration, *Houston*, 86; Davis, *Houston*, 19–20.

85. Frisbee, *Frisbee-Frisbie*, 106; J.C. Chew, *Houston Telegraph* 38, no. 43, ed. 1 (Thursday, February 20, 1873) www.texashistory.unt.edu; University of North Texas Libraries, the Portal to Texas History, www.texashistory.unt.edu; crediting the Dolph Briscoe Center for American History. Hoar was part of a large, intelligent, energetic, well-connected, and successful family of formidable people whose achievements would have intimidated a much older man. The Hoar family was based in Concord, Massachusetts, where they are still known as the "Royal Family of Concord." One of Charles's ancestors was the third president of Harvard, and most male members of the family, like Charles, graduated from Harvard. One of his great-grandfathers was Roger Sherman (1721–1793), a signer of the U.S. Declaration of Independence from Connecticut. His father's oldest sister, Elizabeth Sherman Hoar (1814–1878), was engaged to marry Charles Chauncy Emerson, her father's young law partner, Ralph Waldo Emerson's brother, and the namesake of Charles Emerson Hoar. Charles Emerson died of consumption in May 1836, before they were wed. It is not surprising that, following the fiasco that was Houston's second City Hall, Charles Emerson Hoar left Houston in early 1873 and eventually moved to Southern California, where he disappeared into obscurity; "Finding Aids," in "Hoar Family Papers, 1738–1958," www.concordlibrary.org; Fox, "Houston Buildings," 1; "City Engineer," *Houston Telegraph* 38, no. 35 (December 19, 1872), www.texashistory.unt. edu, 5; J.C. Chew, *Houston Telegraph* 38, no. 35, ed. 1 (Thursday, December 19, 1872) www.texashistory.unt.edu; University of North Texas Libraries, the Portal to Texas History, www.texashistory.unt.edu; crediting the Dolph Briscoe Center for American History.

86. Works Progress Administration, *Houston*, 246–48.

87. Ericson and Wallace, "Constitution."

88. Scardino, "Legacy," 154–64; Works Progress Administration, *Houston*, 246–48; Carroll, *History of Houston*, 78–79; Lewis, "Market Square."

89. Fox, "Houston Buildings," 2–23. Duhamel was born in Buffalo, New York. He and his family moved with his father, a French-Canadian builder and contractor, to Wisconsin, Canada, and Chicago. In Houston, Duhamel also designed the fourth Harris County Courthouse (1883–1909) and the Burns Building (1883–1993) at 421 Main Street. He practiced in Houston, Galveston, and Austin before moving to El Paso in 1887. In 1889, Duhamel left Texas to become a contractor and builder in Chicago, Seattle, and Tacoma, Washington. He died in Seattle

in 1911; Jeanson, "Courthouses"; Waymarking, "Market Square Park, Houston, Texas"; *Volume of Memoirs*, 698; *Washingtonians*, 153; Scardino, "Legacy," 154–64; Works Progress Administration, *Houston*, 246–48.

90. "The New Market," *Galveston Daily News*, 11.

91. Young, *Thumb-Nail*, 17.

92. Scardino, "Legacy," 154–64; "The New Market," *Galveston Daily News*. Fulton was known for producing particularly high-quality bells in the foundries it operated in the Pittsburgh area from 1832 to the early 1900s under several different names. Green, *Fire Fighters*, 123.

93. Works Progress Administration, *Houston*, 90.

94. Young, *Thumb-Nail*, 17.

95. Platt, *City Building*, 96–97.

96. City of Houston, "Franchise Administration." Franchise Fees Today: "The City of Houston's Franchise Administration collects franchise fees from electric and gas utilities, municipally franchised cable television providers, commercial solid waste transporters, network facilities franchises…railroad spur track franchises and businesses operating under right-of-way encroachment ordinances"; Platt, *City Building*, 96–103.

97. Young, *Thumb-Nail*, 19–22. Ohio-born Daniel Cargill Smith (1836–1915) moved to Harrisburg, Texas, to work with the Buffalo Bayou, Brazos & Colorado Railroad (BBB&C) in August 1858. He was a trained railroad machinist and engineer who also was a knowledgeable bookkeeper and real estate investor. He served in the Confederate army until the Battle of Vicksburg and "was placed on detail duty as master mechanic" of the BBB&C until the war ended. In Houston, he partnered with B.C. Simpson and C.C. Wiggin, establishing machine shops for them through 1874. After selling his partnership interest, Smith managed the W.G. Bagby Foundry, specializing in large railroad contracts. In 1880, the Southern Pacific Railway appointed him master mechanic for its Louisiana division. After serving as mayor of Houston from 1886 to 1890, Smith was appointed postmaster at Houston in 1893. He was married and had four children. He died on January 13, 1915, and was buried at Glenwood Cemetery; Works Progress Administration, *Houston*, 95.

98. Jones, "Charlotte Allen"; Works Progress Administration, *Houston*, 247; Allen, "Deed," 330–31.

99. Scardino, "Legacy," 154–64; Works Progress Administration, *Houston*, 246–48.

100. Form Swift, "Texas Quit Claim Deed Form," www.formswift.com, "A quit claim deed in the state of Texas is a legal document that is used to convey property from an owner to a seller. These documents transfer the ownership rights to a property *with no warranty or guarantee that the title is clear and free of encumbrances*."; Works Progress Administration, *Houston*, 247–48.

101. Fox, "Dickey." Dickey and his family left Houston after the City Hall complex was finished. He died in Tennessee on February 25, 1910, but was buried in New Orleans. He was a charter member of the Texas State Association of Architects, organized in 1886, and a member of the American Institute of Architects. The

turret, or "Witch's Hat," from Dickey's Allen Paul House (1901–97) at 2201 Fannin Street survived and was incorporated into the 2016 Asakura Robinson–designed the Park for Humans and Dogs at 901 Sawyer Street in the Old Sixth Ward. One of the Paul House's many tenants was a dance studio owned by Patsy Swayze, whose son, Patrick, grew up to play a *Ghost*; Ancestry, "George E. Dickey, Certificate of Death"; *History of Texas*, 509–10; Tommaney, "Witch's Hat."

102. Genealogy, "Clark Gable," www.genealogy.com. Maria "Ria" Franklin Prentiss Lucas Langham Gable (1884–1966) was born in Kentucky on January 17, 1884, and died in Houston in 1966. She was the second wife of both Thomas Lucas and Clark Gable. Ria married Gable on July 19, 1931, and gave him a friendly divorce in March 1939. She is buried in the Lucas plot at Glenwood Cemetery; NNDB, "Clark Gable," www.nndb.com; Strom, *Lost and Unbuilt*, 69–73; "'A City of Fine Buildings,'" *Houston Chronicle*, 31.

103. Indiana Department of Natural Resources, "Romanesque." Romanesque-era (800–1150 CE) architecture was "popular for large-scale public buildings, such as courthouses, city halls, train depots, and churches....The single most characteristic feature of the style is the use of heavy masonry (brick or roughly finished stone) walls pierced by massive, multiple coursed round arches"; Carroll, *History of Houston*, 399–400; Scardino, "Legacy," 154–64; Strom, *Lost and Unbuilt*, 69–73.

104. "'A City of Fine Buildings,'" *Houston Chronicle*, 31; Carroll, *History of Houston*, 399–400; Scardino, "Legacy," 154–64; Strom, *Lost and Unbuilt*, 69–73.

105. Ibid.; "Mayor's Office, Mayoral History," www.houstontx.gov. Photographs of most of Houston's mayors are on the City of Houston's website.

106. Carroll, *History of Houston*, 399–400; Scardino, "Legacy," 154–64; Strom, *Lost and Unbuilt*, 69–73.

107. In *Fire Fighters of Houston, 1838–1915*, Green described "a larger and finer-toned bell, which today designates the hours as told by the faces of the clock that look north, east, south and west from the tall tower," 123; "Clock's Days Numbered," *Houston Chronicle*; Works Progress Administration, *Houston*, 247.

108. Cotham, "Dick Dowling Statue." The Dowling Monument Association was created to coordinate public fundraising. The eight-foot-high statue stood on a twenty-foot-tall granite pedestal that was incised with the names of the Confederate soldiers who took part in the Battle of Sabine Pass.

109. Scardino, "Legacy," 154–64; Works Progress Administration, *Houston*, 248.

110. Works Progress Administration, *Houston*, 248.

111. The cenotaph, Houston's primary World War I memorial, was sponsored by the Houston War Mothers; Lewis, "Market Square."

112. Works Progress Administration, *Houston*, 248.

113. Ibid.; Chapman, "Downtown Civic Center." Both the Dick Dowling statue and the World War I cenotaph were moved to Sam Houston Park in 1939. The Dowling statue was moved again from Sam Houston Park to a triangle of land near the Cambridge Street entrance to Hermann Park in 1958. On June 18, 2020, it was removed from Hermann Park and placed in storage; Deborah Wrigley, "Statue of Confederate Commander Dick Dowling Removed from

Hermann Park," aired by *ABC Eyewitness News* on June 18, 2010, www.abc13.com; Digital Exhibit of the Dick Dowling Archive, "Dick Dowling and Sabine Pass in History and Memory," Woodson Research Center, Fondren Library, Rice University, www.exhibits.library.rice.edu.

114. Chapman, "Downtown Civic Center"; Lord, *Discover Houston*.

115. Works Progress Administration, *Houston*, 248; *Houston City Directory, 1940*, 1506.

116. Works Progress Administration, *Houston*, 285–86; "Old City Hall," *Houston Chronicle*, 10; "Allen Heirs," *Houston Press*.

117. "Man Is Shot to Death," *Houston Chronicle*, 1.

118. "Houston Wins," *Houston Chronicle*.

119. "Landmark Damaged," *Houston Chronicle*; "Clock's Days Numbered," *Houston Chronicle*.

120. Bertelsen, "Feels Like a Million."

121. United States Census Bureau, "Table 19"; United States Census Bureau, "Table 24."

122. Sabota, "Market Square."

123. NAWCC San Jacinto Chapter 139, "Tower Clock."

124. "Found Among Ruins," *Houston Chronicle*.

125. "Old Fire Bell?" *Houston Chronicle*.

126. "'Old Lady,'" *Houston Chronicle*.

127. "Improvement Gets Under Way," *Houston Chronicle*.

128. "Vote Reported Light," *Houston Chronicle*; Theis, "Back to the Future," 22–29.

129. Ibid.; Minnette Boesel, "Historic Preservation in Houston," *Houston Review of History and Culture* 3, no. 2 (Spring 2006), www.houstonhistorymagazine.org. This article provides an excellent history of Houston's historic preservation movement.

130. In 1969, the City of Houston covered 453 square miles and had a population of 1.3 million, making it the nation's sixth-largest city. Fifty years later, Houston encompassed 665 square miles and had a population of 2.31 million. A.J. Mistretta, "Houston in 1969: A Look at the City Then and Now," *Greater Houston Partnership*, July 1, 2019, www.houston.org.

131. Ann Holmes, "Greening of Old Market Square in the Works," *Houston Chronicle*, Tuesday, March 9, 1976, accessed August 12, 2019, www.infoweb.newsbank.com.

132. In 2010, the marker was moved to the corner of Travis and Congress Streets.

133. Betty Chapman, "Historic City Clock Regained Place in Old Market Square," Historic Houston, *Houston Business Journal*, June 18, 2004; "Houston Retains Legal Title to Historic City Hall Clock," *Houston Chronicle*, January 17, 1979, accessed August 15, 2019, www.infoweb.newsbank.com.

134. Barlow, "City Hall Clock,"; "Retains Legal Title," *Houston Chronicle*.

135. Barlow, "City Hall Clock,"; "Retains Legal Title," *Houston Chronicle*.

136. Ibid.; Tutt, "Come Home"; Chapman, "Historic City Clock."

137. National Register of Historic Places Inventory, Main Street and Market Square Historic District nomination form, July 18, 1983.

138. Theis, "Back to the Future," 22–29.

139. Barlow, "City Hall Clock."

140. Holmes, "Funding."

141. Huber, "Market Square Park."

142. Holmes, "Funding."

143. Tutt, "Come Home."

144. "Cleaning Time," *Houston Chronicle*.

145. Boesel, "Historic Preservation," 7; "Market Square Designation," *Downtown Magazine*.

146. Makeig, "Clock Story."

147. "The Market Square Park Project" Brochure, 1985; Leslie Sowers, "Past Present in Park," *Houston Chronicle*, August 13, 1991; Kathy Williams, "Modern History," *Houston Chronicle*, July 1, 1992, 1, 4.

148. Houston Parks and Recreation Department, "Park." In 2012, members of San Jacinto Chapter 139 of the National Association of Watch and Clock Collectors (NAWCC) took photographs of the Friedman Clock Tower and of the Seth Thomas clock's mechanism and posted them on their website. The website also has a link to Jim West's Videos, including "The Case of the Disappearing Clock," a video that relates the adventures of the clock and bell; San Jacinto Chapter 139, "National Association of Watch and Clock Collectors," www.chapter139.com; Clifford Pugh, "On the Square," *Houston Chronicle*, June 30, 2004, 13.

149. Julie Mason, "Council Grants Market Square Special Taxing Status," *Houston Chronicle*, December 14, 1995. The Tax Increment Reinvestment Zone (TIRZ) froze taxes within the zone for thirty years (2025). As new development occurred, the additional tax revenue it generated was collected for reinvestment directly within district boundaries. The Downtown Redevelopment Authority oversaw development and public improvements within the district. Houston's first two TIRZs were created for Lamar Terrace in Uptown Houston and Midtown on the southern edge of downtown.

150. "Area Briefs, Historic District," Houston Chronicle, March 6, 1997, 26, www.infoweb.newsbank.com.

151. Johnson, Annual Financial Report.

152. "Face Lift," *Houston Chronicle*; The Houston Downtown Management District was created in 1995.

153. Milling, "Art Center?"

154. Lauren Griffith Associates, www.laurengriffithassociates.com; Kerry Goelzer, www.kerrygoelzerassociates.com.

155. "Face Lift," *Houston Chronicle*; Boesel, "Historic Preservation."

156. Houston BCycle, www.houstonbcycle.com, is a "bike sharing" program members and non-members can use for short trips in and around downtown Houston and surrounding urban areas. With Houston BCycle, you can pick up a bike at any B-station and return it to that same station or any other B-station when you're done.

157. Huber, "Market Square Park"; Lauren Griffith Associates.

158. Lauren Griffith Associates.

159. Lauren Griffith Associates; Kerry Goelzer.
160. "Slogans for War," *Morning Herald* (Uniontown, Pennsylvania), March 3, 1942, accessed August 19, 2019, www.Newspapers.com.

Chapter 2

161. Carroll, *History of Houston*, 442.
162. According to one of Sam Houston's biographers, Marquis James, at the ceremony held at Commerce and Main Streets on the first anniversary of the Battle of San Jacinto, "the president accepted a silk flag sent to him by the ladies of New Orleans. He ordered it displayed from the liberty pole as the signal for the procession to march to the scene of the exercises....It was time to march, but the signal flag had not appeared. Fifteen minutes passed, and the column was getting impatient when, finally, the emblem of the Lone Star was broken out against the sky. The delay had been due to the fouling of the halyards. A seaman from a vessel in the bayou had risked his neck to climb the peeled sapling and hoist the gift ensign to its place of honor. After the ceremonies, Houston called the soldier aside and gave him a deed to a town lot. A speculator [Robert Wilson] had recently given the lot to Houston," *The Raven: A Biography of Sam Houston*, 283.
163. Audubon was accompanied by his younger son, John Woodhouse Audubon (1812–1862), and his friend and patron, the Quaker Edward Harris II (1799–1864). Their visit would have occurred between May 1 and May 15, 1837, according to our modern calendar; Maggie Burch, "What Is a Dogtrot House?" *Southern Living*, n.d., www.southernliving.com. "Dogtrot homes are characterized by the large, open breezeway that runs through the middle of the house, with two separate living areas on either side, all under one roof"; James L. Haley, *Sam Houston*, 300. The large, open breezeway and open windows in the separate living areas allowed cooler outside air to circulate through the rooms. According to one of Sam Houston's biographers, "Because of its practicality, it was the most popular style in Texas" in 1837.
164. What Audubon called "dinner" in 1837 we call "lunch" today.
165. Kemp, "Fisher." A native of Philadelphia, Samuel Rhoads Fisher (1794–1839) was appointed secretary of the first Texas navy on October 28, 1836. He was removed from the post on November 28, 1837, by a vote of six-to-five in the Texas Senate on "the grounds of harmony and expediency." He received an honorable discharge since the senate did not find that President Houston had presented enough evidence for a finding of dishonorable conduct. Fisher returned to Matagorda, where he died of a gunshot wound on March 14, 1839. Fisher County, established in 1876, is named for him; Texas History, "The Republic of Texas," www.texashistory.unt.edu.
166. Henson, "Boyce," 30. Robert Boyce was the contractor on the building Audubon visited; "Memoir," 38.
167. Audubon, *John James Audubon, the Naturalist*, 411–13.

168. Audrey Crawford, "A Women's History Tour of Early Houston," a paper prepared for the University of Houston's Summer Seminar for Public School History Teachers, 2002, accessed March 15, 2006, www.discovery.coe.uh.edu.

169. On pages 181 and 182 of their book *Buffalo Bayou*, Louis Aulbach and Linda Gorski write, "With a little imagination, you can…envision a small log cabin [at the intersection of Taft and West Dallas Streets], bounded on the east by a timber post fence, that was recognizable as belonging to Sam Houston's Ranch.…In early 1837, Sam Houston acquired thirty acres west of town on the San Felipe Road…[on which he] established a farm that became known as the 'Houston Ranch.'" An excellent description and maps of the area can be found in Worrall, "Chapter 4: The Town of Houston and the San Felipe Trail After Independence," *Pleasant Bend*, 69–95.

170. "Birthday," *Galveston Daily News*.

171. Williams and Barker, *Writings of Sam Houston*, 182.

172. Holley, *Texas Diary*, 36.

173. Works Progress Administration, *Houston*, 48.

174. Haley, *Sam Houston*, 186, 199.

175. Holley, *Texas Diary*, 36; Wilson, *Native Houstonian*, 30.

176. Williams and Barker, "Writings of Sam Houston," 184.

177. Lubbock, *Six Decades*, 47.

178. Ibid., 66–67; Henson, "Boyce," 30; "Memoir," 38; Stephen Fox, *Houston Architectural Guide*, Third Edition (Houston, TX: AIA Houston and Minor Design, 2012), 39.

179. Williams and Barker, "Writings of Sam Houston," 184.

180. Henson, "Boyce," 30; "Memoir," 38.

181. Henson, "Boyce," 30; "Memoir," 39.

182. Henson, "Boyce," 30; "Memoir," 40.

183. Henson, "Boyce," 30; "Memoir," 40–41.

184. Seale, *Houston's Wife*, 55.

185. Henson, "Boyce," 30; "Memoir," 43.

186. According to Carl Jillson in *Lone Star Tarnished: A Critical Look at Texas Politics and Public Policy* (9), "The terms of Texas's admission to the union in December 1845 were highly favorable and brought badly needed financial relief. Five million dollars in Republic of Texas debts were assumed by the federal government and Texas retained title to all of its unsettled lands to offset its remaining debts. After admission to the union, disputes over the boundaries between Texas, New Mexico, and Colorado, provided another opportunity for Texas to benefit. In the Boundary Act of 1850, Senator Sam Houston and the Texas congressional delegation agreed to limit Texas's claims in the Upper Rio Grande in exchange for a payment to the state of $10 million. Debts quickly devoured this $10 million, but a second payment of $7.5 million in 1855, as a final debt payment and reimbursement of state expenditures for frontier defense, left Texas not only debt free for the first time but with a bankable surplus of $4 million."

187. Henson, "Boyce," 31; "Memoir," 43.

188. Koch, *Houston, Texas, in 1873*. In this illustration from the 1873 bird's-eye-view map, Houston's second City Hall takes up an entire block (Block 34) between Congress and Preston Streets, facing Travis Street and bears the number "2." The street behind City Hall is Milam, and the block to the south of Block 34 is Block 43.

189. Henson, "Boyce," 31; "Memoir," 43.

190. Henson, "Boyce," 31; "Memoir," 44.

191. Henson, "Boyce," 31; "Memoir," 44.

192. Young, *True Stories*.

193. History, "Juneteenth." "On June 19, 1865, two months after the surrender of Confederate General Robert E. Lee…Union General Gordon Granger and approximately 1,800 federal troops arrived in Galveston, Texas, to take control of the state and enforce the Emancipation Proclamation [of 1863]. Granger read General Order No. 3, which declared, in part: 'The people of Texas are informed that, in accordance with a proclamation from the Executive of the United States, all slaves are free.' Juneteenth (short for 'June Nineteenth') is a holiday commemorating this day, which marked the effective end of slavery in the United States.…In 1979, Texas became the first state to make Juneteenth an official holiday, and today, most states hold Juneteenth observances." The City of Houston celebrates Juneteenth annually at Emancipation Park, 3018 Emancipation Boulevard, in the Third Ward.

194. Ancestry, "Hardcastle"; Aulbach and Gorski, "Freedmanstown"; *Houston City Directory*, 1866; Blandin, *Shearn Church*, 176.

195. Ancestry, "Hardcastle"; Aulbach and Gorski, "Freedmanstown"; Blandin, *Shearn Church*.

196. Aulbach and Gorski, "Freedmanstown."

197. Ibid.

198. Lord, *Discovering Houston*. Houston's city government has gone through a number of changes since 1904. Today, there are sixteen councilmembers; five are elected at large and eleven are elected from specific districts.

199. Wilson, *Alfred C. Finn*, 3. Alfred C. Finn (1883–1964) designed the Pilgrim Building during his "golden period." He was already well known for his work on the Rice Hotel (Rice, 909 Texas Avenue) in 1913. Ahead of him lay commissions for the Gulf Building (Great Jones Building, 712 Main Street) in 1929 and the San Jacinto Monument in 1939; Fox, "Finn."

200. Byrd, "Chapter 3: Catfish Reef," 82–83.

201. Bullard, *Invisible Houston*, 14.

202. The Downtown Houston Tunnel System is one of Houston's best-kept secrets. Set about twenty feet below Houston's downtown street system, the seven-mile tunnel is a series of air-conditioned, mostly private underground passageways, which, with aboveground skywalks, link more than ninety buildings to hotels, banks, corporations, government offices, restaurants, retail stores, and the Theater District. Building property owners maintain security by placing guards at strategic locations throughout the tunnel and by installing cameras to monitor

pedestrian traffic. The tunnel is open during regular business hours, Monday through Friday. It is closed at night, on weekends, and on national holidays. Downtown Houston (www.DowntownHouston.org) publishes several maps online, including an excellent interactive map.

203. Hardtack is a biscuit made from flour, water, and sometimes salt. Inexpensive and long-lasting, it was a staple for soldiers during long military campaigns.

204. "Le Carafe," *Houston Chronicle.*

205. Legacy, "Berry."

206. Racine, "Business as Usual."

207. Ibid.

208. "Tragic Death," *Houston Post.*

209. "Dose of Acid," *Houston Post.* Phenol (carbolic acid) is one of the oldest antiseptic agents but it is also a deadly poison. Joseph Lister (1827–1912) pioneered its use in antiseptic surgery and wound care in England in 1865. He first suspected it would prove an adequate disinfectant because it was used to ease the stench from fields irrigated with sewage waste without harming the livestock. At the beginning of the twentieth century, carbolic acid was sold as a common household disinfectant. It also was commonly used in suicidal acts. In 1904, a Minneapolis coroner noted that there had been one hundred suicides in his city in the last three years, fifty-nine by carbolic acid. He called for tighter regulation of the substance. By the 1920s, closer regulation of carbolic acid greatly reduced the number of suicides by this method. Alcohol neutralizes carbolic acid; Cebula, "Carbolic Acid"; Wikipedia, "Phenol."

210. Wikipedia, "Joseph Lister"; Birdwell, "Brews"; Hauck, *National Directory.*

211. City of Houston Archeological and Historical Commission, "Fox-Kuhlman Building," Landmark and Protected Landmark Designation Report, January 30, 2008, www.houstontx.gov.

212. Ibid.

213. "Charles Stephanes," 264; Texas Underground, "Charles Stephanes."

214. Ibid.

215. City of Houston Archeological and Historical Commission, "Fox-Kuhlman Building," Landmark and Protected Landmark Designation Report, January 30, 2008, www.houstontx.gov.

216. Ibid.

217. Ibid.

218. Ibid.

219. Ibid.

220. Ibid.

221. Palmer, *Palmer List.*

222. Wikipedia, "Nicolaus Copernicus."

223. Wikipedia, "Saxon Lutheran Immigration." During the middle of the nineteenth century, Confessional Lutherans (Orthodox or Old Lutherans) were forced to merge with other Protestant groups into united churches that were easier for the governments of Germany's many kingdoms to control. This "unionism" led to "the

persecution and suppression of the confessional beliefs of orthodox Lutherans" and to German emigration. The Saxony Emigration Society's first voyage took place in November 1838. Five sailing vessels, including the *Copernicus*, were chartered and sailed out of Bremen with between one hundred and two hundred emigrants on each ship. The group arrived in New Orleans in December then traveled by steamboat to St. Louis, Missouri. Louisa and her children were part of a later voyage that arrived in New Orleans on November 18, 1839; "Port of New Orleans, Cleared," *Commercial Bulletin, Price-Current and Shipping List*.

224. Worrall, *Pleasant Bend*, 113–72; City of Houston Archaeological and Historical Commission, "The American Brakeshoe Company Building," Landmark Designation Report, May 22, 2014, www.houstontx.gov.

225. Worrall, *Pleasant Bend*, 118.

226. Headright grants were land grants reserved for men who had immigrated to Texas prior to the Texas Revolution.

227. Tiling, *German Element*, 49; Worrall, *Pleasant Bend*, 118.

228. "Clements' Corner," *Washington Cemetery Historic Trust Newsletter* 25, no. 3 (August 2001).

229. Worrall, *Pleasant Bend*, 118.

230. Lich, *German Texans*, 46; Looscan, "Beginnings of Harris County," 52, 60–61.

231. "Clements' Corner," *Washington Cemetery Historic Trust*.

232. Worrall, *Pleasant Bend*, 118, 283.

233. *Houston City Directory, 1892–1893*, 102, 250, 300; *Houston City Directory, 1926*, 2037; Roberts & Wilk Hardware Company advertisement, 223.

234. Theis, "Back to the Future," 22–29.

235. Mesinger, "Big City Beat."

236. NASA, "Apollo 11 Mission Overview"; Wikipedia, "Apollo 11"; Wikipedia, "Neil Armstrong"; Fishman, "Apollo 11."

237. Charles Fishman, "The Apollo 11 Astronauts Went on a World Tour When t\ They Got Home From the Moon—And It Was More Surreal than Beatlemania," *Fast Company*, www.fastcompany.com.

238. NASA, "Apollo 11 Mission Overview." The family's statement prompted many responses, including the Twitter hashtag "#WinkAtTheMoon"; Wikipedia, "Apollo 11"; Wikipedia, "Neil Armstrong." Schmalbruch, "Glass-Bottomed Sky Pool."

239. Market Square Tower, "Tallest Pool."

240. Schmalbruch, "Glass-Bottomed Sky Pool."

241. "Ali Baba Appears," *Houston Chronicle*, April 14, 1967, https://infoweb.newsbank.com, 24; *Houston Chronicle*, September 21, 1977, https://infoweb.newsbank.com; "Rounding the Square," *Houston Chronicle*, June 8, 1979, https://infoweb.newsbank.com, 107.

242. Barbara Karkabi, "Market Square Memories, Potential Still Thriving," *Houston Chronicle*, November 26, 1982, https://infoweb.newsbank.com, 114–115.

243. Racine, "Business as Usual."

244. Houston Architecture, "Oldest Bar in Houston."

245. Racine, "Business as Usual."

246. Theis, "Back to the Future," 22–29.

247. City of Houston Archaeological and Historical Commission, "Baker-Meyer Building," Protected Landmark Designation Report, June 17, 2010, www. houstontx.gov.

248. Ibid.

249. *History of Texas*, 443–44.

250. Wallis and Hill, *Sixty Years*, 78–79.

251. *History of Texas*, 443–44.

252. Heritage Society at Sam Houston Park, www.heritagesociety.org. Tours of the San Felipe Cottage are available through the Heritage Society at Sam Houston Park, 1100 Bagby Street.

253. City of Houston Archaeological and Historical Commission, "Baker-Meyer Building," Protected Landmark Designation Report, June 17, 2010, www. houstontx.gov. "Three generations of the Meyer family were instrumental in the development of the Meyerland subdivision, located in southwest Houston west of Post Oak Road and south of the City of Bellaire."

254. *Houston City Directory, 1877–1878*, 108; City of Houston Archaeological and Historical Commission, "Baker-Meyer Building," Protected Landmark Designation Report, June 17, 2010, www.houstontx.gov. "The wide band of trim beneath the cornice is an almost universal feature of Greek Revival buildings. Commonly, the band is made up of undecorated boards, but complex incised decorations also occur, as is seen in the Baker-Meyer Building."

255. Fowler, "Old Market Square," 65. Chapman, "Early Merchants."

256. Treebeards, www.treebeards.com. Treebeards has four other locations in downtown Houston. Find a Grave. "Braun."

257. Shelton, Rodriguez, Feagin, Bullard, and Thomas, *Houston*, 10.

258. Chapman, "Early Merchants."

259. Find a Grave, "Braun."

260. Sweany, "Dirty Thirty."

261. Berkowitz, "Ghost Town"; Wodarski and Wodarski, *Texas Guide*, 117–18.

262. YouTube, "Treebeards Restaurant, Houston, 39 Ghost Hunters," www.youtube.com.

BIBLIOGRAPHY

Abram, Lynwood. "Late-Night Move Called Cowardly/Savings Firm Demolishes 120-Year-Old Bethje-Lang Building." *Houston Chronicle*, March 22, 1988.

Albert and Ethel Herzstein Library, San Jacinto Museum of History. "Lapham, Moses, 1808–1838." Veteran Biographies. www.sanjacinto-museum.org.

Allen, C.M. "Deed to the City of Houston." Deed Book 78. Harris County Archives. Houston, Harris County Clerk's Office.

Ancestry. "Dickey, George E. Certificate of Death. Davidson, Tennessee. City Death Records, Tennessee, 1910." www.ancestry.com.

———. "Hardcastle, Robert." www.ancestry.com.

Architectural Styles of America and Europe. "American Architectural Styles: An Introduction." www.architecturestyles.org.

Audubon, Lucy B., ed. *The Life of John James Audubon, the Naturalist.* New York: G.P. Putnam & Sons, 1870.

Aulbach, Louis F., and Linda Gorski. *Buffalo Bayou: An Echo of Houston's Wilderness Beginnings.* Scotts Valley, CA: CreateSpace Independent Publishing Platform, 2011.

Barker, Eugene C., and James W. Pohl. "Texas Revolution." *Handbook of Texas Online.* www.tshaonline.org.

Barlow, Jim. "Old City Hall Clock." *Houston Chronicle*, August 5, 1982. www.infoweb. newsbank.com.

Berkowitz, Lana. "Downtown Houston Can Be a Real Ghost Town." *Houston Chronicle*, October 21, 2007. www.chron.com.

Bertelsen, Ethel. "Houston Feels Like a Million." *Houston Chronicle*, July 4, 1954.

Birdwell, Scott. "Brews Deserve a Ghost of a Chance." *Houston Chronicle*, October 15, 1999.

Blandin, I.M.E. *History of Shearn Church, 1837–1907.* Houston, TX: J.V. Dealy Company, 1908.

Boesel, Minnette. "Historic Preservation in Houston." *Houston Review of History and Culture* 3, no. 2 (Spring 2006). www.houstonhistorymagazine.org.

Borden, G., and T.H. Borden. "Journals of the Senate and House of the Republic of Texas, First Congress, First Session." *Telegraph and Texas Register*, 1836. www.texashistory.unt.edu.

———. *Telegraph and Texas Register* 1, no. 49, eds. 1 and 3 (Tuesday, December 27, 1836). www.texashistory.unt.edu.

Brasseaux, Carl A., and Keith P. Fontenot. *Steamboats on Louisiana's Bayous: A History and Directory.* Baton Rouge: Louisiana State University Press, 2004.

Bullard, Robert D. *Invisible Houston: The Black Experience in Boom and Bust.* College Station: Texas A&M University Press, 1987.

Byrd, Sig. *Sig Byrd's Houston.* New York: Viking Press, 1955.

Carroll, Benajah Harvey, ed. *Standard History of Houston, Texas, from a Study of the Original Sources.* Knoxville, TN: H.W. Crew & Co., 1912.

Cebula, Larry. "Of Carbolic Acid, Suicide, and Key Words." *Northwest History,* July 5, 2016. www.northwesthistory.blogspot.com.

Chapman, Betty. "Early Merchants Helped Houston Make Fashion Statement." *Houston Business Journal*, March 18, 2007.

———. "Historic City Clock Regained Place in Old Market Square." *Houston Business Journal,* June 18, 2004.

———. "Modern Downtown Civic Center Extends Far Beyond Early Vision." *Houston Business Journal,* September 22, 2006.

"Charles Stephanes." In *Daughters of the Republic of Texas.* New York City: Turner Publishing Company, 1995. www.books.google.com.

Cherry, Mary Alys. "50th Anniversary of Webster City Incorporation." *Houston Chronicle*, April 21, 2008.

Chew, J.C. *Houston Telegraph.* www.texashistory.unt.edu.

City of Houston. "Franchise Administration." www.houstontx.gov.

———. "Reinermann Family." www.houstontx.gov.

City of Houston Archaeological and Historical Commission. "Baker-Meyer Building." Protected Landmark Designation Report, June 17, 2010. www.houstontx.gov.

———. "City of Houston Fire Station No. 11, 4520 Washington Avenue." Protected Landmark Designation Report, February 23, 2006. www.houstontx.gov.

———. "Fox-Kuhlman Building." Landmark Report, January 30, 2008. www.houstontx.gov.

"Clements' Corner." *Washington Cemetery Historic Trust* 25, no. 3 (August 2001). www.washingtoncemetery.org.

Commercial Bulletin, Price-Current and Shipping List. "Port of New Orleans, Cleared." November 23, 1839. www.newspapers.com.

Concord Library. "Hoar Family Papers, 1738–1958." www.concordlibrary.org.

Cotham, Edward T., Jr. "Dick Dowling Statue." *Texas Escapes.* www.texasescapes.com.

Crawford, Audrey. "A Women's History Tour of Early Houston." A Paper Prepared for the University of Houston's Summer Seminar for Public School History Teachers, 2002. http://discovery.coe.uh.edu.

Cruger and Moore. *Telegraph and Texas Register.* www.texashistory.unt.edu.

Cushing, E.H. "The City." *Houston Tri-Weekly Telegraph* 31, no. 45 (July 7, 1865). www.texashistory.unt.edu.

Davie, Flora Agatha. *Early History of Houston, Texas, 1836–1845.* Austin, TX: n.p., 1940. www.archive.org.

Davis, John L. *Houston: A Historical Portrait.* Austin, TX: Encino Press, 1983.

Dittman, Ralph E. *Allen's Landing.* Houston, TX: A.C. & J.K. Publisher, 1986.

Downtown Magazine. "City Applies for Market Square Designation." January 1991.

Ericson, Joe E., and Ernest Wallace. "Constitution of 1876." Handbook of Texas Online. www.tshaonline.org.

Farrar, R.M. *The Story of Buffalo Bayou and the Houston Ship Channel.* Houston, TX: Chamber of Commerce, 1926. www.texashistory.unt.edu.

Find a Grave. "Braun, Ruth Sacks." Obituary. www.findagrave.com.

Fishman, Charles. "The Apollo 11 Astronauts Went on a World Tour When They Got Home from the Moon—And It Was More Surreal than Beatlemania." *Fast Company.* www.fastcompany.com.

Foner, Eric. "Civil War and Reconstruction, 1861–1877." Gilder Lehrman Institute of American History AP US History Study Guide. www.ap.gilderlehrman.org.

Form Swift. "Texas Quit Claim Deed Form." www.formswift.com.

Fowler, Ed. "Old Market Square. It Lived on Hope, It's Dying of Greed." *Houston Chronicle,* October 5, 1975. www.infoweb.newsbank.com.

Fox, Stephen. "Dickey, George E." Handbook of Texas Online. www.tshaonline. org.

———."Finn, Alfred Charles." *Handbook of Texas Online.* www.tshaonline.org.

———. *Houston Architectural Guide.* 3rd ed. Houston, TX: AIA Houston and Minor Design, 2012.

———. "The Houston Buildings of Nicholas Clayton." *The Houston Review* 9, no. 1 (1987). www.houstonhistorymagazine.org.

Frantz, Joe B., ed. "Moses Lapham: His Life and Some Selected Correspondence." *Southwestern Historical Quarterly* 54 (April 1951).

Frisbee, Edward Selah. *The Frisbee-Frisbie Genealogy.* Rutland, VT: Tuttle Company, 1926. www.archive.org.

Galicki, Marta. "Why Do We Stay in Houston? A Personal History of Three Momentous Arrivals." www.mail.google.com.

Galveston Daily News. "Eighty-Ninth Birthday." 53, no. 114 (July 15, 1894). www. texashistory.unt.edu.

———. "Houston Local." July 18, 1871. www.newspapers.com.

———. "The New Market." November 9, 1877. www.newspaperarchive.com.

Galveston Island Guide. "Phillips, James: Inshore Sculpture, Original Wood Carvings." www.galvestonislandguide.com.

Gammel, Hans Peter Mareus Neilsen. *The Laws of Texas, 1822–1897.* Vol. 1. Austin, TX: University of North Texas Libraries, 1898. www.texashistory.unt.edu.

Genealogy. "Gable, Clark." www.genealogy.com.

Glass, James L. "The Original Book of Sales of Lots of the Houston Town Company from 1835 Forward." *Houston Review* 16, no. 3 (1994).

Green, Charles D. *Fire Fighters of Houston, 1838–1915*. Houston, TX: Dealy-Adey, 1915. www.archive.org.

Hafertepe, Kenneth. *A History of the French Legation in Texas*. Austin: Texas State Historical Association, 1989.

Harris County Clerk's Office. Deed Records of Harris County, A.

Hauck, Dennis William. *The National Directory of Haunted Places*. New York: Penguin Random House, 1999.

Henson, Margaret S. "Robert P. Boyce: Nineteenth-Century Houstonian." *Houston Review* 6, no. 1 (1984).

Hinton, Marks. *Historic Houston Streets*. Houston: Archival Press of Texas, 2006.

History of Texas, Together with a Biographical History of the Cities of Houston and Galveston. Chicago: Lewis Publishing Co., 1895. www.archive.org.

Holley, Joe. "Allen Brothers: The Wheeling-Dealing Duo Who Turned Mud to Gold." *Houston Chronicle*, May 19, 2016. www.houstonchronicle.com.

Holley, Mary Austin. *Texas Diary, 1835–1838*, edited J.P. Bryan. Austin: University of Texas Press, 1965.

Holman, James S. "Unreserved Sale of Houston City Lots." *Telegraph and Texas Register* 2, no. 30 (August 12, 1837). www.texashistory.unt.edu.

Holmes, Ann. "Funding for Market Square Park Project Hits Halfway Mark." *Houston Chronicle*, March 17, 1989.

———. "Greening of Old Market Square in the Works." *Houston Chronicle*, March 9, 1976. www.infoweb.newsbank.com.

Houston Architecture. "Oldest Bar in Houston." www.houstonarchitecture.com.

Houston BCycle. www.houstonbcycle.com.

Houston Chronicle. "Claim to Old City Hall Block Again Pressed." May 5, 1940. www.newsbank.com.

———. "Cleaning Time." August 7, 1990. www.infoweb.newsbank.com.

———. "Houston Retains Legal Title to Historic City Hall Clock." January 17, 1979. www.infoweb.newsbank.com.

———. "Houston Wins in Old City Hall Case." February 6, 1946. www.infoweb.newsbank.com.

———. "Landmark Damaged in Spectacular Fire." April 20, 1946. www.infoweb.newsbank.com.

———. "Le Carafe Offers Snack, Atmosphere." June 18, 1962. www.infoweb.newsbank.com.

———. "Man Is Shot to Death by His Stepson: Thomas P. Converse Slain Following Argument with Wife Over Letter; Cab Driver Charged." July 19, 1943. www.infoweb.newsbank.com.

———. "Market Square Face Lift Slated to Begin This Week." July 16, 1997.

———. "Old City Fire Bell Found Among Ruins." May 25, 1960. www.infoweb.newsbank.com.

———. "Old City Hall Clock's Days Numbered." April 27, 1948. www.infoweb.newsbank.com.

————. "'Old Lady Was a Power in Her Day, but Time, Fate Did Her In." July 31, 1960. www.infoweb.newsbank.com.

————. "Old Market Square Improvement Gets Under Way with $65,000." September 4, 1963. www.infoweb.newsbank.com.

————. "Old Market Square Vote Reported Light." July 22, 1961. www.infoweb.newsbank.com.

————. "Where Is Old Fire Bell?" October 22, 1967. www.infoweb.newsbank.com.

————. "Will Be 'A City of Fine Buildings.'" October 14, 1903. www.public.maximus.newsbank.com.

Houston City Directory, 1866. Compiled by W.A. Leonard. Houston, TX: Gray, Strickland & Co., 1866.

Houston City Directory, 1877–1878. Houston, TX: W.M. Hamilton, 1877.

Houston City Directory, 1892–1893. Houston, TX: Morrison and Fourmey Directory Co. Inc., 1893.

Houston City Directory, 1917. Houston, TX: Morrison and Fourmey Directory Co. Inc., 1917.

Houston City Directory, 1926. Houston, TX: Morrison and Fourmey Directory Co. Inc., 1926.

Houston City Directory, 1940. Houston, TX: Morrison and Fourmey Directory Co. Inc., 1940.

Houston Parks and Recreation Department. "Market Square Park." www.houstontx.gov.

Houston Post. "Allen Heirs Claim Old City Hall." May 4, 1940.

————. "A Double Dose of Acid." May 6, 1910. www.newspapers.com.

Howe-Houghton, Dorothy Knox, Barrie M. Scardino, Sadie Gwin Blackburn, and Katherine S. Howe. *Houston's Forgotten Heritage: Landscape, Houses, Interiors, 1824–1914.* A Project of the Junior League of Houston Inc. Houston, TX: Rice University Press, 1991.

Huber, Kathy. "Market Square Park." *Houston Chronicle*, December 23, 1990.

Indiana Department of Natural Resources. "Romanesque Revival Style." www.in.gov.

James, Marquis. *The Raven: A Biography of Sam Houston.* Indianapolis: Bobbs-Merrill, 1929.

Jeanson, Terry. "The Courthouses of Harris County." *Texas Escapes Online Magazine*, August 28, 2011. www.texasescapes.com.

Jillson, Carl. *Lone Star Tarnished: A Critical Look at Texas Politics and Public Policy.* New York: Routledge, Taylor and Francis Group, 2015.

Jim West Videos. "The Case of the Disappearing Clock." www.youtube.com.

Johnson, Judy Gray, city controller. *Comprehensive Annual Financial Report for the Fiscal Year Ended June 30, 2003.* Houston, TX: Office of the City Controller, December 23, 2003. www.houstontx.gov.

Johnston, Marguerite. *Houston: The Unknown City, 1836–1946.* College Station: Texas A&M Press, 1991.

Jones, Nancy Baker. "Allen, Charlotte Marie Baldwin." *Handbook of Texas Online.* www.tshaonline.org.

Karkabi, Barbara. "Market Square Memories, Potential Still Thriving." *Houston Chronicle*, November 26, 1982. www.infoweb.newsbank.com.

Kemp, L.W. "Fisher, Samuel Rhoads." *Handbook of Texas Online*. www.tshaonline.org.

Kerry Goelzer Associates. www.kerrygoelzerassociates.com.

Koch, Augustus. *Houston, Texas, in 1873. Bird's Eye View of the City of Houston, Texas 1873*, 1873. Lithograph (hand-colored), 23.2 x 30.1 in. Published by J.J. Stoner, Madison, Wisconsin, Center for American History, University of Texas at Austin. www.commons.wikimedia.org.

Lauren Griffith Associates. www.laurengriffithassociates.com.

Legacy. "Berry, William." Obituary. www.legacy.com.

Legislative Reference Library of Texas. *Journals of the House of Representatives of the Republic of Texas, First Congress, First Session*. Houston: *Telegraph and Texas Register*, 1838. www.lrl.texas.gov.

Lewis, Pamela. "Market Square as Old as Houston." *Houston Post*, May 5, 1989.

Lich, Glen E. *The German Texans*. San Antonio: Institute of Texan Cultures, University of Texas at San Antonio, 1996.

Looscan, Adele B. "IV. The Beginnings of Houston, Harris County, 1822–1845." *Southwestern Historical Quarterly* 19, no. 1 (July 1915).

Lord, Sandra. *Discover Houston Downtown: The Theater District*. Houston, TX: CitiWalks Press, 2019.

———. *Discovering Houston: The Six Historic Wards*. Houston, TX: CitiWalks Press, 2020.

Lubbock, Francis Richard. *Six Decades in Texas; or, Memoirs of Francis Richard Lubbock, Governor of Texas in War Time, a Personal Experience in Business, War, and Politics*. Austin, TX: B.C. Jones & Co., 1900. www.lccn.loc.gov.

MacCorquodale, Ellen Douglas. "Houston's Purchase Price." *Civics for Houston* 1 (February 1928).

Makeig, John. "Clock Story Just Won't End." *Houston Chronicle*, July 8, 1995.

Market Square Park Project. Houston, TX: Self-published, 1985.

Market Square Tower. "Tallest Pool in Texas." www.marketsquaretower.com.

Mason, Julie. "Council Grants Market Square Special Taxing Status." *Houston Chronicle*, December 14, 1995.

McCoy, Nancy T., and David G. Woodcock. *Architecture That Speaks*. College Station: Texas A&M University Press, 2017.

McGinty, Jean Epperson. "Steamboat Served Republic of Texas as Floating Capitol." *Port of Houston Magazine* 25, no. 4 (April 1981).

Merseburger, Marion. "A Political History of Houston, Texas, During the Reconstruction Period as Recorded by the Press, 1868–1873." Master's thesis, Rice Institute, May 1950. www.scholarship.rice.edu.

Mesinger, Maxine. "Big City Beat." *Houston Chronicle*, August 4, 1969. www.infoweb.newsbank.com.

Milling, T.J. "Market Square as Art Center?" *Houston Chronicle*, July 6, 1991.

Mistretta, A.J. "Houston in 1969: A Look at the City Then and Now." *Greater Houston Partnership*, July 1, 2019. www.houston.org.

Moneyhon, Carl. *Republicanism in Reconstruction Texas.* College Station: Texas A&M Press, 1980.

Moore, Barry. "Past Forward: How Houston's Preservation Movement Turned the Corner." OffCite. www.offcite.org.

Morning Herald. "Slogans for War." March 3, 1942. www.newspapers.com.

Nance, Joseph Milton. "Republic of Texas." *Handbook of Texas Online.* www.tshaonline.org.

NASA. "Apollo 11 Mission Overview." www.nasa.gov.

National Register of Historic Places. www.nps.gov.

National Register of Historic Places Inventory. Main Street and Market Square Historic District nomination form. July 18, 1983.

NAWCC San Jacinto Chapter 139. "City Hall Tower Clock." www.chapter139.com.

Neighborhoods. "Six Historic Wards of Houston." www.neighborhoods.com.

New English Dictionary on Historical Principles. Oxford, UK: Clarendon Press, 1910.

NNDB. "Gable, Clark." www.nndb.com.

Official Data Foundation. "Consumer Price Index Calculator." www.officialdata.org.

Palmer, Michael P. *Palmer List of Merchant Vessels.* Claremont, CA.: Michael Palmer, 2000. www.oocities.org.

Platt, Harold L. *City Building in the New South: The Growth of Public Services in Houston, Texas, 1830–1915.* Philadelphia: Temple University Press, 1983.

Pugh, Clifford. "On the Square." *Houston Chronicle,* June 30, 2004.

Racine, Marty. "Business as Usual at Downtown Watering Holes." *Houston Chronicle,* October 20, 2002.

Roark, Wanda Louisa. "Robert Wilson: Letters to His Son." Master's thesis, Stephen F. Austin State College, 1966.

Robert P. Boyce Collection. "Memoir of Robert P. Boyce." Houston Metropolitan Research Center, Houston Public Library.

Roberts, Madge Thornall. *The Personal Correspondence of Sam Houston 1839–1845.* Vol. 1. Denton: University of North Texas Press, 1996.

Robinson, Willard B. "Temples of Knowledge: Historic Mains of Texas Colleges and Universities." *Southwestern Historical Quarterly* 77, no. 4 (1974). www.jstor.org.

Sabota, Danni. "Market Square, 300 Block of Travis Street." *Houston Business Journal,* May 5, 1992.

San Jacinto Chapter 139. "National Association of Watch and Clock Collectors." www.chapter139.com.

Scardino, Barrie. "A Legacy of City Halls for Houston." *Houston Review* 4, no. 3 (Fall 1982).

Schermerhorn, Jack Lawrence, and Calvin Schermerhorn. *The Business of Slavery and the Rise of American Capitalism, 1815–1860.* New Haven, CT: Yale University Press, 2015.

Schmalbruch, Sarah. "A Glass-Bottomed Sky Pool Just Opened in Houston—And It's Both Terrifying and Amazing." www.insider.com.

Seale, William. *Sam Houston's Wife: A Biography of Margaret Lea Houston.* Norman: University of Oklahoma Press, 1970.

Shelton, Ruth Anne, Nestor P. Rodriguez, Joe R. Feagin, Robert D. Bullard, and Robert D. Thomas. *Houston: Growth and Decline in a Sunbelt Boomtown*. Comparative American Cities Series. Philadelphia: Temple University Press, 1989.

Sketches of Washingtonians. Seattle: Wellington C. Wolfe & Co., 1906.

Southwick, Leslie H. "The Texas Presidential Election of 1838: Robert Wilson." *Houston Review* 13, no. 1 (1991). www.houstonhistorymagazine.org.

Sowers, Leslie. "Past Present in Park." *Houston Chronicle*, August 13, 1991.

Strom, Steven R. *Houston Lost and Unbuilt*. Austin: University of Texas Press, 2010.

Sweany, Brian D. "Dirty Thirty." *Texas Monthly*, September 2001. www.texasmonthly.com.

Texas Almanac. "National Capitals of Texas." www.texasalmanac.com.

Texas History. "The Republic of Texas." www.texashistory.unt.edu.

Texas State Historical Association. "Austin, John Punderson." Handbook of Texas Online. www.tshaonline.org.

———. "Texas Day by Day: September 5th, 1836—Sam Houston Elected First President of the Republic of Texas." www.texasdaybyday.com.

Texas Underground. "Charles Stephanes." www.thetexasunderground.blogspot.com.

Theis, David. "Back to the Future." *Downtown*, September 2, 2010.

Tiling, Moritz. *The German Element in Texas from 1820 to 1850*. Houston, TX: Reinand Sons, 1913.

Tommaney, Susie. "Houston's Witch's Hat Finds a New Home." *Houston Press*, August 26, 2016. www.houstonpress.com.

"Tragic Death," *Houston Post* 20, no. 82 (June 25, 1904). www.texashistory.unt.edu.

Tutt, Bob. "Time to Come Home." *Houston Chronicle*, February 17, 1988. www.infoweb.newsbank.com.

United States Census Bureau. "Table 19. Cities with 100,000 Inhabitants or More in 1960—Population, 1910 to 1960, and Area, 1960." Section 1, population, Statistical Abstract of the United States: 1970. www.census.gov.

———. "Table 24. Cities with 100,000 Inhabitants or More in 1970—Population, 1950 to 1977, and Area, 1970." Section 1, population, Statistical Abstract of the United States: 1980. www.census.gov.

A Volume of Memoirs and Genealogy of Representative Citizens of the City of Seattle and County of King, Washington. New York and Chicago: Lewis Publishing Co., 1903.

Wagner, Janet K. "Harrisburg and John Richardson Harris." Harris County Towns and Cities. www.historicalcommission.harriscountytx.gov.

Wallis, Jonnie Lockhart, and Laurence L. Hill. *Sixty Years on the Brazos: The Life and Letters of Dr. John Washington Lockhart*. Los Angeles: Dunn Bros., 1930.

Washington-on-the-Brazos State Historical Foundation. "Republic of Texas Capitals." Where Texas Became Texas. www.wheretexasbecametexas.org.

Waymarking. "Market Square Park, Houston, Texas." www.waymarking.com.

Wikipedia. "Apollo 11." www.wikipedia.org.

———. "Bateau." www.wikipedia.org.

———. "Joseph Lister." www.wikipedia.org.

———. "Long Expedition." www.wikipedia.org.

———. "McGowan, Alexander." www.wikipedia.org.

———. "Mill (grinding)." www.wikipedia.org.

———. "Morris, John Robert." www.wikipedia.org.

———. "Neil Armstrong." www.wikipedia.org.

———. "Nicolaus Copernicus." www.wikipedia.org.

———. "Phenol." www.wikipedia.org.

———. "Saw Pit." www.wikipedia.org.

———. "Saxon Lutheran Immigration, 1838–1839." www.wikipedia.org.

———. "Steamboats of the Mississippi River." www.wikipedia.org.

Williams, Amelia W. "Allen, Augustus Chapman." *Handbook of Texas Online.* www.tshaonline.org.

Williams, Amelia W., and Eugene C. Barker, eds. "Houston to Robert A. Irion, January 23, 1837." In *The Writings of Sam Houston 1813–1863.* Vol. 2. Austin: University of Texas Press, 1939.

Williams, Kathy. "Modern History." *Houston Chronicle,* July 1, 1992.

Wilson, Ann Quin. *Native Houstonian: A Collective Portrait.* Norfolk/Virginia Beach, VA: Donning Company, 1922.

Wilson, Michael. *Alfred C. Finn: Builder of Houston.* Houston, TX: Houston Public Library, 1983.

Winkler, Ernest William. "The Seat of Government of Texas." *Texas Historical Association Quarterly* 10, no. 2 (October 1906).

Wodarski, Robert, and Ann Powell Wodarski. *Texas Guide to Haunted Restaurants, Taverns, and Inns.* Lanham, MD: Republic of Texas Press, 2001.

Worrall, Dan Michael. *Pleasant Bend: Upper Buffalo Bayou and the San Felipe Trail in the Nineteenth Century.* Houston, TX: Concertina Press, 2016.

Writers' Program, Works Progress Administration in the State of Texas. *Houston: A History and Guide.* American Guide Series. Houston, TX: Anson Jones Press, Harris County Historical Society Inc., 1942.

Young, Dr. S.O. *A Thumb-Nail History of the City of Houston, Texas.* Houston, TX: Rice University, 2007. www.scholarship.rice.edu.

———. *True Stories of Old Houston and Houstonians.* Galveston, TX: Oscar Springer, 1913. www.archive.org.

ABOUT THE AUTHORS

Sandra Lord (www.houstonwalks.us) is a writer and avocational historian. A native of Pittsburgh, Pennsylvania, she is a graduate of Smith College in Northhampton, Massachusetts. She spent her junior year abroad in Geneva, Switzerland, and has lived in France, England, Washington, D.C., Philadelphia, New Jersey, Rhode Island, New York, Montana, Alaska, and California. Over the years, she has written and edited more than one hundred articles and books for private clients, the University of Pittsburgh, and the University of Houston. Since moving to Houston in 1984, she has been actively involved in learning more about her adopted hometown. She was a founding member of the Professional Tour Guide Association of Houston, the Friends of the Texas Room, and the Houston History Association. Between 1988 and 2016, she conducted guided tours through her companies, Discover Houston Tours and Houston Urban Adventures. Now retired, she researches and writes about Houston.

Debe Branning (www.facebook.com/DebeBranning) has been the director of the MVD Ghostchasers, a Mesa and Bisbee, Arizona–based paranormal team, since 1994. The team conducts investigations of haunted and historical locations throughout Arizona and has

offered paranormal workshops and investigations since 2002. Debe has talked about historic and haunted Arizona as a guest lecturer and speaker at Arizona universities and community colleges, science fiction and paranormal conferences, historical societies, and libraries. Her television appearances have included an episode of *Streets of Fear* for www.fearnet.com (2009), an episode of the Travel Channel's *Ghost Stories* about haunted Jerome, Arizona (2010), and an episode of *Ghost Adventures: Old Gila County Jail and Courthouse* (2018). As a paranormal travel journalist, she has investigated haunted locations, including castles, jails, ships, inns, and cemeteries, and has taken walking ghost tours in the United States, England, Scotland, Ireland, and Mexico. She has been a guest of the Historic Hotels of the Rockies and U.S. tourism departments in Carlsbad, Salem, and Biloxi. A preservation activist with a special interest in preserving historic cemeteries, Debe serves on the board of directors of the Pioneers' Cemetery Association and the Arizona Genealogical Advisory Board and is one of the cohosts of the Association of Gravestones Studies in Arizona. Debe is also the author of *Sleeping with Ghosts: A Ghost Hunter's Guide to Arizona's Haunted Hotels and Inns* (2004), *Grand Canyon Ghost Stories* (2012), *The Graveyard Shift: Arizona's Historic and Haunted Cemeteries* (2012), *Dining with the Dead: Arizona's Historic and Haunted Restaurants and Cafés* (2017), and *Haunted Phoenix* (Arcadia, 2019). She also created The Adventures of Chickolet Pigolet, a series of three children's books: *The Bribe of Frankenbeans*, *Murmer on the Oink Express*, and *You Ought to Be in Pig-tures*.